Praise for
Lead WITH FAITH

"In *Lead with FAITH*, Sarah Johnson empowers readers to live aligned with their own story and to lead confidently in faith at work, at home, and in life. She helps us uncover deeply rooted connections between foundational leadership and spiritual truths. By eloquently and vulnerably sharing her own leap of faith, Johnson will inspire readers to overcome fear and slay their personal giants, by building firm foundations to rise up and bravely, relentlessly, leading with faith, right where they are."

—**Thomas C. Murray**, author of *Personal & Authentic* and director of innovation, Future Ready Schools

"*Lead with FAITH* by Sarah Johnson will push you to reflect on your personal spiritual journey and help you begin to understand your tendencies and appreciate the beauty of your own flaws. Wherever you are on your journey, Johnson will inspire you to lead with more faith and less fear as you affirm your purpose in your daily work and life. The book is filled with vignettes from current practitioners who have shown a commitment to leap past their own fears on their spiritual quest to living a more purposeful life."

—**Jimmy Casas**, educator, author, speaker, and leadership coach

"Sarah Johnson has written a beautiful, soul-moving book. *Lead with FAITH* is full of Scripture, heart-wrenching stories, and useful tools that have readers making connections to their own lives and embarking on a journey of self-reflection. Readers will know Sarah's heart and faith, her flaws and failures, and her intense determination to lead with faith, and it will inspire them to seek more from their own lives."

—**Allyson Apsey**, principal and author of *Through the Lens of Serendipity*

"*Lead with FAITH* is a compass for educators to guide their journey in school and life. Sarah pours her heart out in this manifesto of a life worth leading. Her natural ability to share with humor and humility allows readers a comfortable seat at the table to the journey she takes you on in this book."

—**Jessica Cabeen**, nationally distinguished principal, author, and speaker

"*Lead with FAITH* reads like a warm blanket wrapping you up and comforting you on a cold day. Sarah Johnson intertwines the often-missed factor of faith in one's leadership journey with stories and resources that reflect, build, and strengthen the leadership potential in all of us. Bringing the spiritual element of faith through biblical references helps to discover our true purpose and calling for not only our work but our lives."

—**Neil Gupta, EdD**, district administrator, Ohio

"If you're looking for a book that both inspires and grounds you in your faith while leading in bold and sustainable ways, look no further. This is it! As the 2019 North Dakota Teacher of the Year, a pastor's wife, a keynote speaker, and advocate for kids everywhere, I cannot give *Lead with FAITH* high enough praise. Sarah is a highly talented practitioner, and she has ignited me and equipped me with ideas I've implemented at school, at speaking events, at church, and at home. In *Lead with FAITH*, Sarah quotes Scripture directly from the Bible and connects it practically to modern-day leadership. The spiritual impact has been immediate and profound."

—**Kayla Dornfeld**, 2019 North Dakota Teacher of the Year, author, and CEO, Top Dog Teaching Inc.

"Leadership, in any facet, is a difficult task, and *Lead with FAITH* is the exact book I needed to read. Sarah does a masterful job of showing what authentic and genuine leadership is through her own heartfelt stories of trial and pain. This book is an amazing tool on how to become a faith-based leader and how the Holy Spirit is able to use our gifts, love, and compassion to empower us to lead with a true purpose."

—**Joshua Stamper**, assistant principal, speaker, and host of *Aspire: The Leadership Development Podcast*

"Sarah reminds us that faith is not a passive descriptor, but a verb that allows for deeper relationships to form. Through her faith in the One who called her, Sarah has literally helped save my life, allowed me to understand my purpose, and begin to reacquire a faith that was left dormant for far too long. *Lead with FAITH* is not an answer to leadership; it is *the* answer. By acknowledging your place, your purpose, and your calling, you are able to stand beside others and lead them to where they need to be as well. Sarah, you have helped save destinies with this book. I am grateful for your willingness to respond to the still small voice that challenged you to write it. You, my friend, are an example to all."

—**Dave Schmittou, EdD**, executive director of curriculum and instruction, speaker, and author

"Life is filled with ups and downs, and even more so if you're in a leadership position. It is so incredibly easy to find yourself on a 'hustle and bustle' track just trying to survive work and life, yet knowing you are not at your best. In *Lead with FAITH*, Sarah vulnerably opens up while also sharing stories from other leaders to help you see that you are not alone. She will take you on a journey to reclaim the core of yourself so that you too can *Lead with FAITH*."

—**Jessica Johnson**, principal and coauthor of *Balance Like a Pirate*

"Sarah Johnson is on a mission to help us all make a bigger impact on the people we lead. In *Lead with FAITH*, Sarah guides readers through a journey of self-discovery and a deep dive into spiritual beliefs. Sarah's inspiring personal story is integrated throughout the book to illustrate the power of faith-driven leadership. The path may be long, but Sarah reveals the beauty of leaning on His strength through the hills and valleys. This book provides the encouragement leaders need to keep praying and keep slaying."
—**Julie Hasson, EdD,** Nina B. Hollis Endowed Chair in Education at Florida Southern College, founder of Chalk and Chances, author of *Unmapped Potential*

"As I read and reread *Lead with FAITH*, this love letter to a Higher Power kept bringing me back to the root of servant leadership: a loving relationship with our God, alongside a faith family that will nourish us spiritually so we can positively influence and inspire as we help others fight their fears and live wholeheartedly. From knowing yourself to honoring your strengths, from recognizing your areas for growth to setting self-improvement intentions, this comprehensive leadership manifesto seamlessly weaves Sarah's personal experience as a teacher, a mom, a wife, a principal, and an entrepreneur into wisdom and resources from educators in the field that'll help us lead and grow. Thank you, Sarah, for sharing this vulnerably raw and refreshingly transparent look into your passionate run from fear-based hanging on to faith-based living strong."

—**Barbara Gruener**, counselor, speaker, author of *What's Under Your Cape?*

Lead
WITH
FAITH

BUILDING A STRONG FOUNDATION
SO YOU CAN RISE UP, SLAY FEAR, AND SERVE WELL

SARAH L. JOHNSON

Lead with FAITH

© 2019 by Sarah L. Johnson

All rights are reserved. No part of this publication may be reproduced in any form or by any electronic or mechanical means, including information storage and retrieval systems, without permission in writing by the publisher, except by a reviewer who may quote brief passages in a review. For information regarding permission, contact the publisher at info@courageousheartpress.com.

> These books are available at special discounts when purchased in bulk for use as premiums, promotions, fundraising, or group studies. For inquiries and details, contact: info@courageousheartpress.

Published by Courageous Heart Press
Cover design by Genesis Kohler

Scripture quotations taken from The Holy Bible, New International Version® NIV®, ©1973 1978 1984 2011 by Biblica, Inc. TM Used by permission. All rights reserved worldwide.

Scripture quotations marked NLT are taken from the Holy Bible, New Living Translation, ©1996, 2004, 2015 by Tyndale House Foundation. Used by permission of Tyndale House Publishers, Inc., Carol Stream, Illinois 60188. All rights reserved.

Scripture taken from the New King James Version®, ©1982 by Thomas Nelson. Used by permission. All rights reserved.

Library of Congress Control Number: On File
Paperback ISBN: 978-1-950714-01-8
eBook ISBN: 978-1-950714-02-5

I lovingly dedicate this book to Selene and Adelle. May you remember forever how grateful I am that God let me be your earthly mother. Live free to be who God made you, affirmed in your unique purpose, be intentional about the time and gifts you've been given, embrace transformation into your best versions, and never forget to lead with your wonderful hearts.

I love you more than all the moons and stars in all the planets in all the galaxies in all the solar systems.

Contents

Foreword by Dwight Carter xi

My Faith Story xv

From Rising to Slaying xix

1 Leading with Faith ~~Over~~ Through Fear 1

2 Leading with FAITH 5

Section One: Leading *Free* to Be You 9

   3 The Need for Self-Awareness 19

   4 Leading with Your Signature Strengths 33

Section Two: Purpose in Leadership *Affirmed* 51

   5 Leading from Your Core Values 59

   6 Determine Your Mission and Vision 71

Section Three: *Intentionality* to Inspire and Influence Others 79

   7 Immersing Yourself in Your Full Life 85

   8 Make Each Day Count 93

   9 Practice Gratitude to Inspire and Build Up Others 107

Section Four: *Transcend* Titles and Embrace *Transformation* ... 121

   10 Servant Leadership or Martyrdom? 127

   11 Leadership That Transforms 137

Section Five: Leading with *Heart* 147

   12 Wholehearted Living 155

   13 Emotional Intelligence and Empathy 171

Conclusion: Rise Up from the Pit 183

Foreword

BY DWIGHT CARTER, SCHOOL LEADER

Faith is the substance of things hoped for and the evidence of things unseen.

—Hebrews 11:1

Hebrews 11:1 is arguably one of the most meaningful and misunderstood scriptures in the Bible. Faith is not blind allegiance to the unknown, but an intentional belief in something based on experience. It takes courage, conviction, discipline, and a desire to live with faith because it's something that is questioned daily. Faith is not ignorant; it is knowing. Faith is not idle; it is doing. Faith is an action word.

I first met Sarah in the registration line at the National Association of Secondary School Principals annual conference in July 2018. She was behind me in line, and our first interaction involved her asking me if I thought she would get kicked out if she tried to register two other people. Though we had never met, she acted as if we were friends. She seemed a bit anxious, and when she got to the front, I leaned in and said, "Umm, I think they are getting security right now." She nervously chuckled, and I laughed. "I'm just joking." We both laughed and parted ways, she with her extra registration bags, and I to my room to ready for dinner with friends. I honestly expected never to see her again at this large conference. To my surprise, Sarah was part of the dinner party gathered that evening with her friend and coauthor of *Balance Like a Pirate,* Jessica Johnson. Sarah had failed to mention she was an author and presenter!

I attended Sarah and her coauthors' session and was amazed by her journey. In the midst of a successful career as a high school principal, she heard the call of the Holy Spirit to walk away from the principalship and to "lead the masses." With no plan in place, just clarity and conviction, she resigned. Just like that.

I had my doubts about one just leaving with no plan, so after the session, I approached her to ask more questions and to share a little bit of my story about leaving the principalship. She shared more about her journey, and it was then that I was convinced that she sincerely "walks by faith and not by sight."

Sarah and I stayed in touch through social media. When she launched her *In AWE Podcast*, I quickly subscribed. I enjoy listening to the voices she amplifies on this platform, which is simply an example of how her faith is lived with intentionality and purpose. As she continues to live out her faith, she followed the nudging of the Holy Spirit and penned *Lead with FAITH.*

It can be difficult in today's polarized and humanist world to declare one's faith with a strong conviction because of how easily it can offend others. It is equally challenging to do so as a public school employee, especially as a school leader. Because of the difficulties that come with leadership and the current "Cancel Culture" in which we live, it can be much easier for leaders to keep our faith safely packed away at home. To do so is not leading with faith, but living in fear. Sarah Johnson tackles this issue with grace, patience, and humility as she opens her heart to beautifully weave her faith journey into each chapter—a journey that includes her failings and stumbles, her fears, and her victories over fear. As you walk alongside her through each chapter, you will notice how her conviction to lead with faith strengthens as she describes the FAITH framework she created while studying the life of King David. Faith is knowing and doing. Faith is an action word.

Sarah combines the power of the biblical Scripture, research-based personal development assessments, the latest research on shame and vulnerability, and authentic stories to provide a pathway to how one can lead with faith. The message is not preachy but practical. It's not condescending but convincing that it's okay and necessary to be faith-filled as a leader. It's not an indictment but an invitation to be your authentic self. It's not a proclamation of perfection but a pathway to vulnerability. Sometimes we need to hear a voice in the wilderness of doubt, fatigue, fear, or apathy, so Sarah includes the stories of several leaders to share their personal testimonies of how they lead with faith, which provides even more encouragement and "the evidence of things unseen."

Many leaders understand what they need to do and why they need to do it, which is to create the conditions for students and staff or those they lead in any organization to be successful, but the question that this book answers is how to do it in the midst of today's culture while being true to oneself. Authentic leadership is a necessity and can transform schools into vibrant, relationship-oriented, and high-achieving institutions of learning. I applaud Sarah's boldness and courage to tell her story, sharing both her experience and the experience of others who successfully lead with faith.

Be Great,
Dwight Carter, school leader

My Faith Story

Faith isn't about having everything figured out ahead of time; faith is about following the quiet voice of God without having everything figured out ahead of time.
—Rachel Held Evans

On January 11, 2018, as I sat listening quietly to the still, small voice of the Holy Spirit, I received direction with such conviction and love, my heart still pounds recalling the peace within the words spoken: "It is time to fortify your spirit and clothe yourself in Me, to raise your voice in praise of what we have done together." Though there are many messages in that entry in my journal, and hundreds since to continue to speak life into my actions to rise with God's purpose in me, that phrase encapsulates the catalyst for my leap of faith to lead with faith. My faith walk means my voice must amplify beyond my journal to praise the good work that God has done in me, even when I feel inadequate for the task. When I look back at the pivotal message, I am reminded that none of my best contributions to this world come from my own strength; therefore, I can move forward with confidence to share what God has done *for* me, knowing He will continue to work *through* me.

My faith journey as I understand it today informs much of the messages weaved together on these pages. My heart lays vulnerably exposed and imperfect through the obedient risk I take in bringing you along with me, knowing my own journey is nowhere near complete. If you choose to read the whole of this text, you will learn I was raised in a traditional Christian home, that I fell away from religion for a time, and understand that I have run back to spirituality with fervent, heart-nourished faith. I am not an expert theologian. The only authority I have comes from my experiences—failings and victories—and, most essentially, from the strength that God provides. Honestly, His presence and leading are more important to me than any degree, affiliation, or endorsement the world would provide. I do not have all the answers, and my representations may be quite flawed in the eyes of others. What I know is that my own understandings continue to deepen, even in the year since taking up the blessed directive to write this book. In her text, *Out of Sorts: Making Peace with an Evolving Faith*, Sarah Bessey speaks comfort to my heart regarding this growth when she observes, "If our theology doesn't shift and change over our lifetimes, then I have to wonder if we're paying attention." Noticing and paying attention and living intentionally with a fervent focus on present moment awareness characterizes much of my most recent chapter in life. This shift has developed my thinking, broadened my understanding beyond my faith upbringing, and deepened my desire to remain connected in loving relationship, waking me up on fire with a commitment to become who God says I am.

The One whose opinion of me is equal parts undeserved and irrational shines vibrantly over every distraction and imperfection, both in my daily routines and in the writing of this project. Even as I type, I pray over it, *May I honor God's love by placing the highest value on His label on my heart, above any other, so that those who would take this message into their hearts would know it was meant to land where they need it.* My faith is firm enough to know in confidence that prayer will be answered in ways I would never think to ask or imagine.

If you do choose to read all of what follows, be ready to see how flawed I am as a person who continues to seek, to learn, and to believe that we are all connected in ways that we may never understand in this life. Maybe it will help you to know that, at times in my life, I have questioned religion, turned away in shame, and felt isolated from the very community meant to help keep me on my faith path. In truth, portions of the Christian *religion* nag at my core and create a dust-up inside my soul. When people of any denomination use sacred texts to marginalize others or rationalize condemning others, my blood boils. In studying all that divides the Christian faith into so many sects, I have come to chasms I didn't know how to overcome on my own. Yet I have learned with other flawed humans who have taken the journey long before me, and in much of what I continue to learn; I am so grateful to know that I am not alone in my seeking. From all of this learning, I continue to come out stronger in my faith, more deeply convicted that my heart is in the right hands. A deep truth I have learned is that wisdom in leadership and faith does not come in the knowing, rather we earn it from the seeking and growing. Explaining my own feelings on faith in the midst of that turmoil in my mind, Rachel Held Evans breathes life into my being with her own declaration. In *Inspired: Slaying Giants, Walking on Water, and Loving the Bible Again*, she writes, "'I am a Christian,' I concluded, 'because the story of Jesus is still the story I'm willing to risk being wrong about.'"

Risk. Writing about my own faith as if it matters to others feels incredibly risky. Boldly professing my love for God, the belief in Jesus Christ as my Savior, and aligning my steps to the actions the Holy Spirit calls feels right. True. The least risky part of this entire project.

Like you, fear grips me, I am tempted, I fail at following all the rules of religion, and, like you, I desire to know more about God's design for my life.

My gratitude that you would come with me in this leap of faith to lead with faith lights the fire in my soul passionately, douses fear in sharing my heart and creates a bold spirit in me to drive forth. May this message be exactly what you need when you need it. Thank you for allowing me to live out my own mission to support you on your journey toward leading with more FAITH and less fear.

From Rising to Slaying

It is this belief in a power larger than myself, and other than myself, which allows me to venture into the unknown and even the unknowable.

—Maya Angelou

You may be wondering, Is *she really writing a book for leaders about faith—and focusing on Christian faith at that?* Of all places, where I led in the public school setting, people seem most concerned about being politically correct, inclusive of all, and determined not to step on anyone's toes. In this setting, faith is a topic into which few dare to venture. And I get it. Our challenging and dynamic experiences, coupled with varied backgrounds and understandings, create intimidating complexity within the concept of faith. For some of us, the more we learn, the more we realize how little we know. As one of my favorite thinkers on this topic, Barbara Brown Taylor asserts in her most recent work *Holy Envy: Finding God in the Faith of Others*, "Even people who belong to the same religion do not agree about what they mean when they say 'God.'" From a scholar who has spent a lifetime learning and teaching about faith, such a simple observation illustrates a tension point for many of us. We may ask, "If there is no universal truth, what is true?"

In my corner of the world, I have observed that fear, in one form or another, often prevents us from talking about our faith. Maybe we are fearful of being judged or lumped into someone else's concept of faith. It could be that we have been the ones standing in judgment—either in a season past or the present—believing that our faith is better, stronger, or more "right" than someone else's. Maybe that fear wells up because we feel unstable in our faith and don't want to let others in on that perceived weakness.

Of course, we also need to be respectful of diverse views of faith and spirituality. In that case, it is a lot easier to avoid the topic altogether, right? Whatever our reasons, faith has become a taboo and off-the-table topic for most of us. My own past contains experiences where I've had to be the leader who enforces policies meant to be inclusive of all—that end up alienating most. In our school communities and in leadership, it is critical we don't impose our beliefs on others. Looking deeper, however, it is easy to observe how we are doing ourselves, and those around us, a major disservice in pretending as if our beliefs don't exist. Our identities are tied up in so much of our faith cultures. To deny we are all beings on a great quest for meaning in life diminishes the individual importance of one of the most basic truth searches we all initiate.

Our public school systems and organizations work hard to avoid faith in conversations.

I am here to argue, however, that leading with faith is a topic of the highest need. In her book, *The Gifts of Imperfection*, Brené Brown writes, "Spirituality is recognizing and celebrating that we are all inextricably connected to each other by a power greater than all of us, and that our connection to that power and to one another is grounded in love and compassion. Practicing spirituality brings a sense of perspective, meaning, and purpose to our lives." If that's true, spirituality is what inextricably ties us to one another. All of us! Through this connection, those of us who wish to lead with faith of the Christian variety understand that we are to see ourselves as Christ's ambassadors. Further, our ministry can ground itself in seeing others as made new through the sacrifice that Jesus made.

> *So from now on we regard no one from a worldly point of view. Though we once regarded Christ in this way, we do so no longer. Therefore, if anyone is in Christ, the new creation has come: The old has gone, the new is here! All this is from God, who reconciled us to himself through Christ and gave us the ministry of reconciliation: that God was reconciling the world to himself in Christ, not counting people's sins against them. And he has committed to us the message of reconciliation. We are therefore Christ's ambassadors, as though God were making his appeal through us. We implore you on Christ's behalf: Be reconciled to God. God made him who had no sin to be sin for us, so that in him we might become the righteousness of God.*
> —*2 Corinthians 5:16-21, NIV*

Maybe it will help you to know that others' beliefs and salvation are not placed on your shoulders in this world. Someone else has that job already, if you believe as I do. We simply need to live the ambassador life—firming our own foundations, seeing others through a reconciled lens, and living in such a way that others cannot ignore there is a light shining through.

I wrote this book to empower and encourage leaders to build and stand strong upon a foundation of faith. You'll notice that many of the stories and examples I share come from the world of education because that is where my own leadership was developed, tested, and honed. I hold a special place in my heart for leaders in the public sector, be it in schools, law enforcement, or social services. In these areas, in particular, leaders are exposed to some of the most horrifying ails of this world, including physical, sexual, and emotional abuse of children. We see the absolute underbelly of the world, with much of the pain emanating from the people we signed up to serve. Our why. Our purpose. We see families decimated by growing addictions to drugs and alcohol, challenged by social media and technology breaking down family time, faced with increasing mental health issues, fighting an outwardly driven need to fit a mold rather than belong, and fueled by a constant barrage of fear-inducing images. These images tell us we are not smart enough, wealthy enough, thin enough, exciting enough, happy enough. It's impossible to ignore the wounds that run so deep, they have cut to the heart of those who turn weapons on the communities we serve.

In a world where we are constantly fed negativity by the media and easy-fix industries, and in a career focused on the high needs of others, it is a moral imperative for leaders to focus on filling their wells before they run dry. When we are exposed to this level of darkness, why do we think it's not important to talk about the way we bolster ourselves and replenish our own spiritual stores to lead strong?

Lead with FAITH examines how leaders are fortifying their own foundations so that they can continue to lead in sustainable and courageous ways. FAITH is an acronym to guide you in developing a firm foundation in self-knowledge, purpose, intention, service, and leading with a whole heart. This practical guide includes real stories from the battlefield and impactful lessons from the pit—from someone who knows what it's like from that fear-filled vantage point—and has risen strong to share messages for your benefit. More than anything, *Lead with FAITH* seeks to equip you with a sense of empowerment so that you, too, can slay whatever fear giants may be in your way and lead strong—the fearless way you were meant to lead, the way in which you want to be remembered.

Faith empowers us to be the boldest version of ourselves. Faith is what enables us courageously slay the fear giants we will inevitably face as leaders. The truth is, not everyone is equipped to handle the challenges and triumphs of leadership. If you feel called to leadership, you will most certainly face struggles, hard choices, and difficult situations. These are all meant for you, and the way you respond to them will make an impact on those you serve in ways you may never even fathom in this lifetime. Your legacy as a faith-driven leader is that your messages of hope land when they need to, where they need to. What a gift you are to the world!

As a leader yourself, maybe you can understand how challenging it would be to leave a position you love in an organization. In 2018, after fifteen years of service in schools, that is a choice I made due to the conviction I felt from the Holy Spirit. I bet you can also imagine my bold leap of faith was hard for many to understand, and part of my own courage involves staying on God's path. Rising up out of a titled position you love has its pain points, and leaving the people and the meaningful work we did together held many for me. Yet the new season in my leadership of supporting and encouraging leaders both in and outside of education continues to fill me with courage to continue forth. For me, this season represents slaying fear giants to overcome my desire to retreat to the comfort of what I have known and keep forging forth on this new path to lead boldly. In the past year, I have been honored to speak to and learn from hundreds of women and men—many of them faith-filled educators and leaders—who have inspired and challenged me. I'm sharing some of their stories in this book. Embracing this season has taken time and patience, and this text represents a bold and obedient step to continue to believe that my former season and the current one in which I lead will have meaning.

By removing myself from one calling to move into another, I am leading with faith at the most intense level and finding there are truths I can share on this topic that might benefit others. Leading a school during some of the most disruptive times in our state and locally taught me that we must cling to faith in order to avoid falling into the pit of fear (or to pull ourselves out of it tenaciously). That pit ultimately leads to not only our own shortfalls but those of whom we lead. My life in leadership has not been perfect. I have led out of fear for a time, and there are many regrets I hold from that space, but there is also redemption in the rise from it. What I have gained from those fear-driven experiences are what ink the pages of this text so that other leaders can know they are not alone, that they can rise out of the pit of fear, and that there are tangible and real steps to leading with faith that anyone can embrace.

Throughout the process of writing this book, I have dreamed who you might be as a reader and faced the challenge of writing it and overcoming my own fears in doing so for the greatest benefit of those of you who are in the pit and need these words to hoist yourselves out. If that's you, know you are not alone, and you can lead boldly once again. For those who have been there and know you don't want to go back but might still need help to fortify yourself in certain areas, I fervently include my heartfelt stories of recovery. Maybe you will use them for yourself, or maybe you will honor this purpose by sharing these pages with someone you know who needs them to come out of fear. For those who have yet to tumble into that fearful, ashen pit, I write with confident belief that there will come a time when you will recall some wisdom you once dismissed in these pages and remember there is someone out there who leaped to help you in that future state. This text is all for you. All of you.

What authority do I have to write a book on leadership and faith? The one I've been given in my identity as a daughter of Christ. It is important to me that you know my faith is not built on the laws of religion that can limit access and focus on rules. My passionate faith is about relationship with my Creator and is firmly grounded in spirit, experience, and constant seeking. I am one who loves all people, not just those who believe what I believe or act how I do. Darn it, I even love those who like Neil Diamond. I cannot help myself. This text will not push you to believe in my spiritual faith. It will show you how my own spiritual faith has lifted me through some challenging times, offered shelter in crazy storms, and provided a hope light for what the future could hold.

I wholeheartedly believe that my own story of rising out of fear and into faith is one I am meant to share with you. At no point will I claim I have all the answers to every challenge you as a leader and person face, or the right action, or how to believe from your space in the world. *I simply have the faith to share this message and believe that, through it, you will produce your own answers in your own time with your own wisdom.*

I do not promise to enlighten you but to ignite you. I promise to engage with willing leaders in a conscientious effort to seek bold, faithful leadership that crushes fear. After all, who wants to stay in a pit of fear when they can rise out with arms wide open into the glorious light of the sun?

Taking time away from leading a building filled with the very souls I love deeply to write this text has been one of the greatest challenges of my life. If I didn't rise up and slay this giant by writing this text for you, however, I wouldn't be leading my own legacy in the way I am called to do. Large pieces of me screamed against this directive for my life. What do I have to say that would matter to others? Isn't my life meant to be a legacy lived each daily in the little things? The answer to that last question has been no since January 2018—no matter how painful it is to internalize. But like most of our lives, this new season is one that will not last, and I know that I will be back in a school leadership role because that has been a promise as well. One of the very real giants I slay as I type this text is the one that taunts me relentlessly about what I am missing by sacrificing my joy in the daily interactions with students and staff. With each stroke of the key, I battle that one back, embracing this new leadership imperative to assist you in your own journey. What an honor!

In this book, I am not trying to write a bestseller, just the message you need when you need it. I also believe this message is not merely from me, just through me. After all, we are all meant to serve and lead in the ways in which we are called, and though I remain surprised my path led here, I gladly take each obediently risky step alongside you. Let's journey together toward what it means to *Lead with FAITH*.

Faithfully,
Sarah Lynn Johnson

CHAPTER 1
Leading with Faith ~~Over~~ Through Fear

I learned that courage was not the absence of fear, but the triumph over it. The brave man is not he who does not feel afraid, but he who conquers that fear.
—Nelson Mandela

For God has not given us a spirit of fear and timidity, but of power, love, and self-discipline.
2 Timothy 1:7, NLT

What scares you? When you are alone with your thoughts, what concerns chip away at your courage as you imagine yourself facing a challenge that literally terrifies you? Leading with faith does not mean an absence of fear; rather, it means using the fear to create the exact right amount of energy to slay the giant. As leaders, we must be willing to face our fears and admit they exist in the first place, otherwise how can we expect others to face theirs? Out on the battlefield of our lives, we will inevitably encounter experiences that frighten us. When we choose to lead with faith through that fear, everyone else sees what real courage is and can follow boldly. What happens when we fall to the fear?

Falling into the pit of fear can happen to the best of us. The downward spiral can be the result of a slow slide or an unexpected and traumatic fall, but when we start leading from the fear-filled depths of that pit, we lose. When we lead with fear, we question every motive of the people around us. We assume negative intent, thinking people are out to get us. We become paranoid and cynical.

If we are leading with fear, we become self-centered, thinking that the tiny perception survey results are what define us or the label others have put on us as leaders are our values. When we lead with fear, we worry constantly about what people will think, how events will turn out, if our goals are lofty enough, or if they are too high. We question everything, and that can be very problematic, considering leaders are thrust in the space of making dozens of decisions in a given day, many of them unpredictable, and most have an impact on others. Leading with fear begins to rot our core values. We cannot lead with fear and be bold at the same time. If we are fearful, we don't take calculated and important risks for our students and staff. We don't try new things for fear of making waves, when we should be the ones manning the dinghy to get others off the sinking ship! When we lead from fear, we lead people into the dark caverns with us, leading in the worst way, toward negativity, loss of hope, and mediocrity. We are called to leadership to be courageous, fearless, willing to fight for our students and staff, and able to overcome adversity, obstacles, distractions, and doubt with the tenacity and power of armed soldiers. So why do so many leaders fall into the pit of fear?

My belief is that we lead out of fear when the foundations upon which we are building our legacy are not solid. Much like stories about building castles on sinking sand instead of firm rock, if we

> We cannot lead with fear and be bold at the same time.

do not build our legacies around our values, missions, and knowing ourselves well, we start to wander in all directions. We begin to allow ourselves to be distracted by items that appear important, when the reality is they are simply distractions. If we are not taking the time to define our values and mission, and to align our actions with those critical guides, we begin to feel shame from steps we take that are outside the realm of our values.

In order to avoid leading with fear, we need to always be self-aware, doing an inventory check of the motivations behind what we are feeling, saying, and doing. We need to have core values that are defined and that people can hold us accountable to when we have lost our own way. We need to allow ourselves to answer to entities outside ourselves, as we can sometimes become our own worst enemies due to self-indulgence or self-doubt. (Ask anyone who has tried to change diet habits alone!). While we cannot allow fear to keep us from our path, we can use it to keep us out of the shadows. I believe this means answering to a higher power and building a deep connection with that power that allows us to go beyond distraction, move forward in redemption from failure, and rise out of the fear pit. For you, it may be surrounding yourself with stronger people who make good choices in life, focus on the positive, and work hard to choose well daily. The point is, we have the option to stay out of the pit and lead with faith through fear—we simply must choose to do so. As Zig Ziglar said, "F-E-A-R has two meanings: 'Forget Everything And Run' or 'Face Everything And Rise.' The choice is yours." What will you choose?

Your journey began when you picked up this book to start armoring up for battle. It won't always be easy; conflicts will continue, and often increase in challenge, but courage-style leadership over comfort-style leadership will always be worth it. One assurance I can make is that it takes a leap of faith to lead with faith. While the span of that leap is different for every one of us, the risk gets all our human hearts pumping. As someone who understands well the anticipation just prior to becoming airborne, I am honored to lift off the ground alongside you on your own leap. Hold my hand, and let's go on three.

One . . .

Two . . .

Three . . .

CHAPTER 2
Leading with FAITH

The secret to life and the greatest success strategy of all is to love all of it and fear none of it.

—Jon Gordon, The Carpenter

As a boy, David rose up and slayed a giant. As a young man, he stepped up with trusting faith to lead as he was called. And he leaned mightily on his faith as he lead his people as a king.

When I felt called to move into new areas of leadership, my faith was what supported that shift. Even though I knew God was convicting me with a directive, I wasn't solid on the direction, and I needed answers regarding where I was to rise.

In the fall of 2018, my church entered into a period of fasting and prayer, and what I discovered in setting my own decision about what I would fast was that I had been wasting time in all that seeking. Instead of fasting food or other items, I would fast one hour of wasted time each day and give it to God. For twenty-one days, I engaged in what I called King's Hour—studying segments of the Bible depending upon where God directed me. Not only did I learn that I was to write this message, but I also gained wisdom, clarity, and fortitude in those hours.

As I dove into the study, I conjured up all the visions I knew about David from the Old Testament, singing and praising God in the Psalms. Worship and singing of God's work in my life has been a lifelong love, so raising my voice seemed to be the easy part! I could relate so well to that vision. As I studied further, it struck me that as I envisioned the praises, raising my own voice in worship, and all that was tied to "rise" for me, I had missed several elements to David's story, especially one of the most crucial with the highest implication for courageous leadership: *David was a giant slayer.*

Rising with God's purpose propelled me into a new chapter, but slaying was a whole new way of leading with a Heart of David. Slaying means that we first have to face the fears lying dormant or appearing distant on the battlefield. Once my giants started revealing themselves in front of me, it was clear that this leap of faith was going to represent way more than simply leaving a position and wandering around until the next came along. Thinking that being public about my faith was slaying the giant and that the rest would be easy was so sweet. So flawed. Going from rising to slaying meant I needed to answer the call of several giants and meet them on their turf. Like David, leading with faith as a shepherd, soldier, servant, and royal all require us to slay in different ways.

In this book and in my own world, giants represent our fears, individualized barriers to test our abilities to conquer each one with strength needed that can only come from spiritual courage. A significant portion of me leading with faith now comes in believing my message for you is worthy. Because God said to me during King's Hour, "I have given you gifts to share with others—now it is time to gift them to the world," I do believe it. Consider the impostor syndrome giant who says I don't know enough about faith and leadership slayed and on the ground, friends.

As my study, prayer, and listening continued, the acronym FAITH became a clear path for me.

Free — Being *free* to lead as your most authentic self

Affirmed — Leading **affirmed** in purpose

Intentional — Leading with **intention** to influence and inspire others

Transformation — Transcending titles and embracing **transformation**

Heart — Leading whole**heart**edly, focusing on emotional intelligence and empathy

FAITH is an acronym for a framework guiding our work to Lead with Faith. Each section includes foundational leadership topics augmented with storied illustrations and resources aligned with the concepts. To start each section, I also included framework foundations. These are the ideas I hope stick with you through each piece of the FAITH framework. At the end of each section, I have included my observations from my study of how David lived the FAITH framework, as well as verses for further review. David is not a perfect example of a leader, and neither am I, nor are you. David, however, makes the FAITH framework vividly visible even thousands of years later, which is definitely a legacy worth examining.

Each chapter will end with prompts to guide your reflection to become firmer in the FAITH framework by facing fears and *slaying* fear. Consider these your call to action, and do not ignore the good work of firming your foundations as you read. I want this text to serve as a reflective tool you can come back to as you transform. Taking time to document your thoughts now will enable you to see your growth, both as you read and as you lead, through whatever is to come on your own journey. More than anything, I pray this message settles into the spaces needed inside each of you so that when you are called to the fight, you will not question the outcome but engage bravely, simply because you know and trust *that* giant was *meant for you.*

SECTION ONE
Leading Free to Be You

Authenticity is a collection of choices that we have to make every day. It's about the choice to show up and be real. The choice to be honest. The choice to let our true selves be seen.

—Brené Brown

Free to Be You Foundations

- If we do not work to understand ourselves intimately and accept who we are created to be as fearfully and wonderfully made individuals, we allow others to determine who we become.
- We lead more boldly when we understand how we operate from our signature strengths as well as our areas of weakness.
- We are able to pivot and lead more effectively when we understand how individuals with personalities and character strengths opposite from our own feel valued.

I have witnessed a loved one take in her last breath and pass from this world, poignantly powerless to stop the transition. In 2008, I spent a lot of time driving the two-hour trek to a hospital in Minnesota where I gathered with my cousin and my family members to sit alongside the bed of my much-loved aunt Pat as she fought through the final stages of death after her battle with breast cancer. We did what we could to make her comfortable and to make sure she felt our love. As we sat with her, we recounted tales of her vivacious and bold spirit; we laughed much—and cried too. Waiting alongside others you love deeply as you watch someone you deeply love pass is an experience that is hard to imagine until you have been in it. Being present in that precious moment when a soul leaves the body and a person you love draws a final breath changes you forever. I was most certainly altered in all the meaningful ways a person can be in that space. Delivering my aunt's eulogy remains an honor that surpasses graduation speeches delivered since that day because she was really something to behold in life and at the end. Even as I consider her impact on my life, I realize what a gift her life was to me. The version of her I knew was never afraid to share her opinion, offer a smile, or enjoy a good laugh. She left a silken, feminine, and fierce imprint on my heart from childhood to now as I recall her beautiful soul. And she also left a daughter, Julie, who was more like a sister to me.

Julie was an only child who devoted her life to pouring her gentle heart of service into others. I spent countless nights at her house as child—endless streams of days playing in the light of her sunshine and watching movies I should not have seen until I was ten years older, drinking Coke from the bottle, and eating ice cream by the carton.

We remained close through the years, sharing and celebrating special moments—from weddings to babies. When I finally had a viable pregnancy, Julie was one of the first people I wanted to tell.

Julie and my sisters, Melissa and Sandra, and I were sitting around the table archiving our memories and photos from Race for the Cure, which we joined as a family every year on Mother's Day. I had slipped the sonogram photo into the stack of pictures as a surprise. Upon its discovery, my sisters effusively shared their excitement, hugging me and squealing with joy. Julie simply smiled nonchalantly, then gave her signature laugh and said, "yep," as if I'd only confirmed what she already knew. Months later, she hosted the most wonderful baby shower. We loved making memories together, and as my girls came along, they became part of our adventures.

When breast cancer claimed its hold on Julie, we all hoped she would beat it. In October 2012, shortly after I had been hired as a principal for the first time, I knew we wouldn't have her long. Even though I felt the weight of my new position and was dealing with the lack of balance it created, I took a weekend to drive out and simply sit with my sister and cousin. Honestly, her presence calmed me. As the months and her illness progressed, I knew she was declining, but I didn't realize how dramatically. Julie continued to be one of the strongest, most stoic ladies I had ever known. Gentle. Unassuming. Never in desire of attention.

When I received the call that, instead of leaving the hospital after a recent health concern, she had collapsed and passed suddenly, I was in an administrative meeting. It was December. In that moment, I tasted bitterness of the debilitating guilt I felt for prioritizing my job. I felt awful for not having seen her since October or going the minute I heard of her hospitalization. She died very close to Christmas, and my husband and I took our daughters to church for the first time locally on Christmas Eve. We had not found a church home and had been wandering for years. I'll always remember how well-behaved they were and the fact that "Breath of Heaven" strained into my ears that night for the second time ever—after hearing it for the first time at her funeral days before.

Visiting Julie's house in subsequent months, I was astonished to see that a message I had left on the whiteboard in her kitchen that October remained there. I like to envision the words bolstering her on the hard days, her eyes focusing in on the strung-together letters in a way that fortified her and reminded her that I loved her so deeply and was grateful to her for the way she had helped mold me into the woman I am today. Just maybe those words stayed there long enough for the memory to surface now as a reminder to me that our words matter to others—they really are all we have in this life by our own end.

One of the quirks I have picked up in leadership to help regulate my emotion and increase my sense of strength for the day has long been dressing in a meaningful color or wearing a particular piece of jewelry. After my aunt and cousin passed, pink was my color of strength. After spending years alongside these matriarchs in my life, the color of courage from the battle that had felled them both made me feel strong and shine with their light—solid through the gales of most days. I purchased a bright pink dress that I wore often that year following. My phone cover was pink. My water bottle was pink. These were all strategic choices not because I loved the color, but because every time I donned a pink-hued item, I knew my heart was stronger for it that day.

I share this background with you so that you will have an emotional connection and a deeper understanding for the error I made by not leading free to be me for a time. In my transition into a new position, I attended a training located at the school I had worked as a teacher. In that physical space, I had learned from two of the best mentors in educational leadership, grew strong core values. Loved people around me. Fundraised for the breast cancer cause with a photo of my sister and nieces that I posted on my classroom door. As I sat in that space I had loved so deeply, my heart got sliced, and the letting go of an authentic piece of me began.

I was advised that there was too much pink in my world. I would not be taken seriously as a woman in leadership, and I needed to start dressing more neutrally and get a black phone case.

Sitting here now, I wish I would have spoken up and shared Pat's light and Julie's spirit. I wish I would have shared my heart and simply explained a core value tied to the splashes of pink on my person and in my office.

But I didn't. Not then. I heeded the advice as if adjusting myself to fit a mold based on the world's stereotypes, was going to matter for my leadership. I heeded it, without regard to how removing my emotionally intelligent and secret strategy for fortification would take its toll.

As someone who understands that we must see the patterns in our lives, it is not surprising to me that I was sitting in that same building again when I began to reclaim my core values after a year of fire-forging experiences. At the end of that year, I interviewed for a superintendent position I had no business striving for in the very district where I taught—the same space I can now pinpoint where I started trying to fit a mold of what the world expected and not who I truly was as a leader. Simply being in that healthy learning community, answering core leadership questions, and reflection led me back after a year of fear.

> *I wish I would have shared my heart and simply explained a core value tied to the splashes of pink on my person and in my office. But I didn't. Not then.*

And I bought *another* pink dress shortly after that.

I chose to illustrate this micro example of how I led, not free to be truly me, because it is an easy way to express the main idea of the entire section. It is not to say we cannot be mindful of the messages our clothing sends. It is not to say we should not be able to adjust our practices when the situation calls. It is not to say we need to stubbornly hold to practices or nuances that are detrimental to us or the organizations we lead. It is to *shout* that to lead well, we must know ourselves, understand our motivations behind our actions, deeply hold to values that matter to us, and be tenacious in not allowing the world to change us; rather, we must seek to change the world around us. We can allow ourselves to be influenced by others, but we must retain power over our own thoughts and be a discerning guardian of our own minds.

> *We can allow ourselves to be influenced by others, but we must retain power over our own thoughts and be a discerning guardian of our own minds.*

The world has a habit of sorting and selecting. We need to remember that we were the ones chosen to write our own story. You can bet that mine will have splashes of pink, and now yellow added for suicide awareness and sunshine. No tidbit of research will ever compete with what makes my own light shine and helps me lead free to be the best version of me.

Self-Awareness Takes Intention and Time

Our self-confidence grows as we lead from a place of self-awareness, knowing we are living in real time the legacy we want to lead. When we understand better why we react the way we do to certain situations, we can be proactive in how we handle conflict or other interactions because we lead with self-knowledge. In education, we often talk about Maslow's Hierarchy of Needs, but what about the pinnacle of self-actualization? We know that our students need to have their basic physiological needs met, that they need to feel safe, that they need to feel like they belong, but do we get to their and our need for a meaningful life? It's okay that we may not reach that with students because, after all, the humanistic theory is really about life span and striving.

Let's spend time together at Maslow's top tier of that hierarchy. Self-actualization is making meaning of our lives and becoming our ideal selves. Self-actualization does not happen by age, but through reflection and self-development. When we get past our basic needs, we are able to focus on becoming the best version of ourselves. I am no psychologist, but it is obvious we are evolving beings with unpredictable life experiences that culminate in the overall picture of who we become. That evolution makes reflection essential. Maybe reflection is something you do naturally. Or maybe, like many people, taking an inventory of your strengths and growth areas is something you do only during formal leadership course or perhaps by taking a Facebook quiz. (And let's examine the reliability on those bad boys!)

When was the last time you dug into your own personality or tendencies? In our ever-changing world, if we are relying upon a Myers-Briggs we took in college, we are denying ourselves the ability to change our minds and thoughts on topics. If we are really to embrace the ever-popular belief in a growth mindset, I believe it means we should also apply that to our own personal and professional identity growth. With each step further down any path of leadership, the stakes become higher and more people become focused on our decisions, actions, and styles. We can be subject to public scrutiny and caught up in the interests of people, groups, and that of our organizations. If we are not careful to be self-aware, we will struggle with being free to be ourselves, and this will cause us to lead out of fear of the unknown. Not knowing ourselves can be the greatest danger of all.

This section will prompt you to get to know yourself in more deep and meaningful ways to be certain that your faithful leadership is rooted at your core. If we want to be our best selves, we need to be free to be the version of ourselves we were created to be, and nobody can do that for us. We must be brave enough to define and refine ourselves and show up as authentically us as possible. This also does not mean pushing our own values on others or that others must accept us for who we are in all our spiritual glory. What it does mean is that we must accept ourselves as we are and work to be the very best versions of ourselves always. Freedom to be ourselves requires us to act boldly at times when the way we handle a situation goes counter to what people expect—or our perception of their expectations. It might also mean that we will have to stand alone at times, a space many leaders fear. Standing alone can make us feel we aren't leading, as we believe the measure of a leader is based upon their followers. In the majority of circumstances leading an organization, that is the case. Sometimes those we lead, however, are not brave enough or quite ready to stand with us. They support silently. In this case, freedom to be yourself means that you are faithful enough in the decision you have made to carry the banner for your school, even when nobody else appears to be around you. Free yourself of what others expect of you to fearlessly exist as wholehearted you.

Free yourself of what others expect of you to fearlessly exist as wholehearted you.

Understanding your own tendencies will also make you a stronger leader because you can better understand others' tendencies during interactions. Ever wonder why it drives you crazy when a coworker sits there thinking before responding? Do you find yourself tapping your toes anxiously to respond when another person is talking too long in a staff meeting? How about when someone jumps over your response while you are thinking, and you feel frustrated at the lack of processing time in a team meeting? The truth is that there are all types of beautiful souls on complicated journeys all around us. We are all wired differently, and knowing what makes us and those around us tick helps us to navigate leading others much better.

It might be tempting to breeze through this section, assuming that you have done all this work. After all, you are in your head all the time. Who knows you better than you? This thinking can be problematic because, while that is true and we do know ourselves better than others know our deep thoughts and desires, we are also the best at deceiving ourselves. Take the time and put in the hard work of defining your best self now so you can strive toward that version of you who leads with the confidence that only comes from embracing your most authentic self. This might mean there is striving that occurs to get there. If that is the case, good for you! That striving means you are digging deep and doing the right work.

Also know that you are not alone in the struggle. I am not currently the best version of myself at this time in my life, not by any close margin, and I have recently done the work in these chapters. There are spaces in the fabric of my character and personality that require refinement, and I am content with knowing I still have work to do. The key is that I am aware of those and ready to strive. For me, my strive involves the daily work of being the most fearless version of myself to shine as the most faithful. It's up to us to become who we were meant to be. Nobody can do that for us. It starts with knowledge.

DAVID LED FREE

As a shepherd, a soldier, and as a king, David knew deeply that he was flawed, yet he led with confidence. In his psalms, we can see that his confidence wasn't in himself but in God. Through his writing and life, we can see just how much he loved, worshipped, and trusted God. Though others tried to change him—Saul attempting to give armor before battle, his wife admonishing him for open worship—David lived free to be himself, knowing that God loved him just as he was made, flaws and all, giving credit to God for his gifts. Knowing that God was always with him empowered David and inspired and guided his worship and service.

And David became more and more powerful, because the Lord Almighty was with him.
—1 Chronicles 11:9, NIV

What more can David say to you for honoring your servant? For you know your servant, Lord. For the sake of your servant and according to your will, you have done this great thing and made known all these great promises.
—1 Chronicles 17:18–19, NIV

CHAPTER 3
The Need for Self-Awareness

Most of us don't know that we don't know who we are. We wear these masks, and we allow masks to be put on us by society, by religion, by family. We allow ourselves to overidentify with some of the fragments that've laid claim to the whole of who we are.
—Chris Heuertz, For the Love Podcast *with Jen Hatmaker*

When was the last time you sat down and really examined who you are—not yourself as a leader but you as a person? I am not talking about identifying your favorite color or animal or any other surface concept. I am talking about taking time to assess your personality, your tendencies, your strengths as a human being wonderfully made and beautifully flawed. We can become self-aware through a variety of formats, but they all take intentionality on our part. We must be able to understand our strengths and our weaknesses so that we can lead from our strengths and grow through our weaknesses. Taking time to engage with your authentic self means that you embrace the real parts, not just the version the world—or your own untruths—have manufactured over time. You know, the unfiltered you. Your true self.

To lead as your most authentic self, you must know your most authentic self. This can be a scary experience for some people. When we engage in self-reflection and take it deeper into self-analysis, we can sometimes unearth realities we don't want to face. But how can we be authentic if we have been hiding in layers? Let's peel some back.

In this chapter, I want to share three tools that have been especially helpful to me in my own journal of self-discovery and personal and professional growth: the Enneagram, Myers-Briggs, and the Four Tendencies assessments.

Enneagram: An Interconnection of Personality Types

The Enneagram is a great place to start the self-reflection process. This accessible, deep tool is one tool I highly recommend. This complex and robust assessment is steeped in spirituality and values the connections and complexities of our diverse human makeup and looks deeply into a person. The Enneagram is versatile and gives you multiple angles for analyzing your own design as a person. Please keep in mind, however, like any other assessment, it cannot completely encapsulate your unique composition. It can help you become more aware of who you are. If you spend time diving deeply into this assessment, you will learn that there are core styles, auxiliary core styles (wings), and an analysis of resourceful and less resourceful tendencies in these spaces. The Wagner Enneagram Personality Style Scales (WEPSS) assessment will also provide an analysis of your responses in more and less stressful conditions. Examining this tool should not be a short, fifteen-minute quiz with a label smacked on you. Taking time to dig into these styles and looking at the variables can be provide incredible insight into the motives that drive your behavior. In the Gathering Stones resource list at the end of this section, I have listed some of my favorite tools and sites that will help you better understand personal and professional partnerships when you begin digging into the Enneagram. You may encounter other Enneagram resources online, but I can tell you from experience that not all resources are equal (or even effective). If you want to make the most of this tool, I recommend going beyond the free, online quizzes.

My first experience with the Enneagram came just prior to my resignation as principal. My pastor at the time recommended this tool when I shared with her that I felt convicted by the Holy Spirit to start a new chapter, but I wasn't sure what to do next. I took her suggestion and delved into the Enneagram. Evaluating myself though the lens of this particular tool, provided me with the strength and a deeper level of self-awareness, something I desperately needed at this critical time of transition. The insights gifted me with clarity, timely affirmation of my strengths, and an opportunity to get real with some of the aspects of my makeup that could be refined. It also shined a light on some hope for the future, knowing there is a lot I can offer to this world with my unique gifts.

Honestly, simply acknowledging the best parts of our character and identifying areas for growth empowers us to battle fear. The Enneagram shows us the depth and combination of our character traits and helps us understand how they play together to form unique beings. Engaging in the reflection and analysis also helps peel back the facades we may have layered on over time and reveal the limitations we have placed on our identities from the wear and tear of life.

> *Simply acknowledging the best parts of our character and identifying areas for growth empowers us to battle fear.*

Fair warning: Uncovering and examining every inch of your character can be bolstering, but it can also be painful, confusing, and even shaming. I get it. One source tells me my core style is the most narcissistic. For someone who believes in valuing others and humility, that is hard to see. I acknowledge that my deep belief that we are all unique, and that God has called me to teach masses, illustrates that I do have a tendency to see myself as important. I certainly see His call on my life as such. I can grapple with that pigeonholing of the Enneagram Style 7, though, because I have spent time diving much deeper into this assessment and understand that it is not rigid, nor does one size of a core seven fit everyone. It is maddeningly complex and insightful! Resist reducing your results to the banal level of identifying straight up as your core style. You are so much more than that! Use your number as a guidepost.

To slake some curiosity for readers who are coming to the Enneagram for the first time in this text, here is a graphic that provides a brief description of the core styles.

The Enneagram with Riso-Hudson Type Names

Any Enneagram assessment you choose from the resources at the end of this section will share deeper analysis of the core styles and will help you dig further into the ways your responses indicate tendencies toward auxiliary styles and break down how you function at your healthiest and most unhealthy. Honestly, it will take more reading for you to do this right. I am still in the process of uncovering my own experiences after more than a year of studying and reading multiple texts. My purpose in here is not to give it all to you but to spark in you a desire to know yourself deeply, to face the pieces of you that need refinement, and to embrace and love who you are at your core. My hope is that you will choose to engage in the process in such a deep way that you will not waiver from the best parts of who you were made to be—and to lead and live fully from that space!

Sarah Sunshine Clouded with Coping:
My Experience with the Enneagram

Rose colored glasses. Pollyanna. Pain avoidance. Narcissist. Scattered. These are all descriptors for the Enneagram style seven that have cut me deeply. Depending upon the source, the main descriptor for a seven is Joyful or Enthusiast. Yet, like all core styles, the seven has attributes that can be healthy and also unhealthy.

The healthy side to seeing the joy in life because I tend to the resourceful has always been the best part of being me. It is truly where I am now in the best version of myself so far; however, the harmful side of seeking the silver lining might be due to refusing to face reality.

My core style is a resourceful seven with resourceful tendencies on the eight auxiliary (or wing). This core has served me through a lot of disruption in leadership and helped me to continue persevering through great challenge. On the surface, results say that sevens avoid pain, but I am here to tell you that I dive in with others in their pain. I have learned to value that space and to be a light. But I can tell you there was a time where my unhealthy tendencies reared their head in my personal life. Without even realizing it, I started escaping with a wine habit through the constant pain I was feeling at home after my brother completed a suicide, my marriage was disintegrating, and school was challenging. For someone who had not in their adult life drank alcohol regularly, this was a change, and I should have seen it for what it was then: coping. But because I am a core seven, I was able to continue to see the joy in the majority of life. It cut deeply when people alluded to my view of life being Pollyanna-ish, but I see now that their perception of me came from their own lens. And that is okay. Happily, I can report that the evolution of my own strengths has come from deep spiritual connection and analyzing my own tendencies so I am careful not to cope. That's my logical eight style coming through! Despite my core style of seven, I am not a whimsical adventurer who cannot complete anything, always moving from project to project, covering over issues, and avoiding pain at all costs. Through self-analysis, I am careful to avoid those tempting default tendencies as I continue to move forward in developing my best self.

One of the best gifts of self-assessment is spending time considering what may have led into forming these core styles. The truth is that there is a lot in my past I have had to overcome. An analysis of Enneagram sevens usually means there is pain in their past that they were taught to overcome or avoid through laughter or "shaking it off."

In reality, my childhood holds a lot of ACEs (Adverse Childhood Experiences), but not the ones people saw. My parents did not divorce, I was fed, and I never suffered physical abuse. My ACEs are the varieties nobody would know until I share. They are the kind that forced me to put on a happy face, only because I could with other supports in place in my life—including a highly spiritual and joyful dad. My ACEs were also the kind where an analysis tells me to begin seeing a therapist now that I have uncovered them in my healthy state of self-awareness. My ACEs include being often in the presence of an alcoholic extended family member, early close deaths to people with whom I was deeply attached, and sexual molestation as a child. These are huge. And you bet they have the power to impact life as a leader in both positive and negative ways.

I give thanks, however, to my Heavenly Father for gifting me with the natural ability to reframe most every situation in which I find myself. This has been a gift, and I realize now it is because I am a joyful seven tending toward the resourceful. I have that level of self-awareness in my tendencies so that I do not gloss over reality or avoid pain.

> *We need to be able to clearly see reality if we are to empower ourselves and others to genuinely and authentically overcome adversities.*

A gift of engaging with the Enneagram tool and pursuing further analysis is reviewing and previewing my actions and reactions to certain scenarios. I ask myself in the challenging moments if I am avoiding pain or facing it. Because this personality type often defers to methods of avoiding pain, I ask myself if I am bravely facing pain or if am I using mechanisms to cope in a healthy or harmful way. We need to be able to clearly see reality if we are to empower ourselves and others to genuinely and authentically overcome adversities. And doing that ourselves is a critical step to leading with faith.

FAITH IN ACTION
JILL MARAS, HIGH SCHOOL PRINCIPAL, ILLINOIS

Sitting beside someone, I sense emotions. I tend to realize when a person is down and needing support and find myself praying for them, not knowing the details. The awareness is so second nature I thought everyone could sense this. My husband, Paul, has a knack for numbers. He can remember figures and manipulate them in his mind. It's so second nature to him that he used to believe that everyone saw numbers the same way.

Paul and I have taken quite a few personality assessments to get to know ourselves and each other. These assessments help us to recognize our differences and to understand just how unrealistic it is (and frustrating for the other person) when I expect him to know how I'm feeling or when he expects me to remember the checking account balance. Each time we learn more about our personalities, we are reminded that our gifts are God-given and unique—and we are called by God to use them.

As parents, it has been fascinating to see the unique combination of personality traits God gifted each of our five children. Recently, we all took the Enneagram test and shared our results with one another. We noted things that were obvious as well as things that surprised us. We realized gifts we have seen one another use and ones we would benefit from tapping into. It helped us understand why each of us react to situations differently and truly helped us love the person God created even more. Understanding one another more fully has been hugely helpful for our family!

The Enneagram was also powerful in the work setting. One year, as we began a new school year, I asked my high school staff to take the Enneagram test. Once we had identified our Enneagram numbers, we gathered by Enneagram number to talk about what our traits brought to the school and what we needed from others to be successful. We gathered by departments and talked about what traits were strengths and which were missing. We discussed the impact that our collective strengths and weaknesses might have on our work and on our students. Through this process, we got to know ourselves, and we got to know one another.

To live and lead, knowing ourselves, is to tap into the person we were created to be. To love others the way we were designed to love, and to do show love in ways people were designed to receive it, is to truly do God's desire.

+++

Myers-Briggs: It's Not Just about Introverts and Extroverts

A number of excellent tools are available for self-analysis. In truth, simply spending time alone asking and answering questions is a great way to get to know yourself. As busy leaders, it is tempting to view this self-reflection time as non-productive, but nothing could be further from the truth. We can't expect others to know us if we don't understand ourselves. I won't spend as much time on the subsequent two inventories, but I highly encourage you to engage with both of them to develop a well-rounded view of yourself. They will all have implications for how you lead in any environment. Let's take a look first at the Myers-Briggs assessment.

Even if you haven't studied this assessment in depth, you are likely very familiar with the first two indicators of I and E or introvert and extrovert. Like any label, it is easy to slap some generalizations on the letters and wear the label either with pride or shame. Our culture, in general, tends to value extroversion. In my training as an educator, I was taught to wait seven seconds for a response to a question. Why is that? Because introverts need processing time! If we jump to call on the quickest voice or the loudest voice, we fail to help all of our learners grow and learn.

Of course, this is no different in a staff meeting or a committee of any kind in adulthood. We all crave to be heard; however, the way in which we want to be heard, as well as what we want to hear and how we want to hear it from our leaders, differs depending upon our personality. Taking the time to learn our own tendencies helps us be better about watching for the opposite in others so we can be our best!

So let's spend some time in the most widely popular personality inventory, the Myers-Briggs Type Indicator. First, let's dispel the fact that it's only about introvert and extrovert. Did you know there are three other whole labels you have been missing if you reduced it to I or E? Let's take a look at some general descriptions of the personality types in the inventory. Once you reexamine this involved, yet simple-to-understand, inventory, you will see it is less about letters and more about categories that make up our personalities.

1. How we gain energy: I-Introvert or E-Extrovert
2. How we take in information: S-Sensing or N-Intuition
3. How we make decisions: T-Thinking or F-Feeling
4. Our lifestyle preference: J-Judging or P-Perceiving

From a leadership standpoint, these categories all carry significant weight for our foundations. Understanding our tendencies in each of these spaces allows us to analyze the way in which we interact with people and information. It helps us to understand why and how we make decisions. If we do not bother with understanding our own tendencies, we run the risk of devaluing those who are made up differently than us. There are sixteen personality styles when combining all of these indicators. No style is better than the other. Each of us brings our unique way of interacting with this world, and understanding ourselves is paramount to better leading the other fifteen categories and wonderful personalities!

> No style is better than the other. Each of us brings our unique way of interacting with this world.

In broad strokes, the world looks at extroverts as being highly engaging, outgoing, and gregarious, and introverts as being reserved, less interactive, hermits. False! If you are a leader who has been operating under this myth, you have missed out on the key points. Introvert and extrovert labels are about how we gain energy, not how we spend it. Leaders can be both, and there should be no shame around either style, yet I encounter people in my work all the time who have literally said to me, "I am an introvert, and there is no shame in that." Exactly! It simply means that, at some point in the day, you must find space to be alone, process, and restore energy. As an extrovert working from home, typing on a computer all day, I must intentionally make time to engage with real people because I derive energy from interaction.

Taking time to inventory yourself in each of these spaces will allow you to set boundaries in your leadership that will protect your energy stores and articulate your decision-making process. It will also assist you in developing proposals that are less about how you like to take in information and more about how the people you lead like to receive information. As a case in point, I recall leading a team for adjusting our schedule, and we just couldn't seem to get the change launched. I realize now that the feedback I was receiving about never feeling like they had enough information was from the sensory-focused introverts. They didn't want the big picture; they wanted to know the details in order to buy in! On the other hand, my intuitive people wanted the vision and were annoyed when we became mired in the details. There is much to delve into with those we lead, and knowing about the styles can provide useful insight. For now, it's time to analyze your own tendencies so you can get firm with yourself and begin to reflect upon how those tendencies aid and challenge you in your own leadership role.

Four Tendencies: What Our Motivations Tell Us about Our Productivity

A key foundation to learn about yourself is discovering how you are motivated when it comes to meeting expectations at home, work, and life. Research, such as the work of Daniel Pink outlined in his book *Drive*, indicates that work environments that focus on autonomy and mastery create the most satisfying conditions for motivation. Likewise, our personality traits factor into and drive our behavior.

The need to assess my own motivational tendencies has never been more glaring to me than when I took on the role of entrepreneur and began writing, podcasting, and completing deep work projects with no accountability other than what I set. There was no boss telling me what to do, no board meeting deadline for a report, no end of the term or other measure of accountability other than the one I set. When I consider the life of a leader in an organization, it fascinates me how much expectation is laid on his or her shoulders, and I wonder about what motivates each of us to complete tasks. If we want to be able to lead others by their strengths, it is critical to understand how we and they are motivated. Knowing what our tendencies are can also make us aware of how we form our expectations for those we lead.

One source that has impacted my own work a great deal recently is Gretchen Rubin's *Four Tendencies*. She has an awesome book and companion website, which allows you to take her tendencies quiz free. In order to understand the tool a bit, here are the four tendencies and just a brief description of each.

Upholders: respond readily to outer and inner expectations

Questioners: question all expectations; they'll meet an expectation if they think it makes sense; essentially, they make all expectations into inner expectations

Obligers: meet outer expectations, but struggle to meet expectations they impose on themselves

Rebels: resist all expectations, outer and inner alike

What I find fascinating about Rubin's work is that it takes the research about motivation and really pares it into the individual person functioning in an organization. Initially, it may seem easy to simply identify yourself under these categories, but I encourage you to engage with the quiz and find out your own tendency. As with any tool, the opportunity to reflect upon your tendencies allows you to determine what you will need to do to begin improving your practice, particularly if your tendency is getting in the way of you facing your fears or leading most effectively.

Face the Fear

As you were reading, did you consider examples of times you felt undervalued for your contributions in an organization due to your personality tendency? Are you a person who feels shame from either being too much or too little with your personality? Sit with this for a minute and consider how a deeper reflection about these experiences will help you lead stronger in the future.

Slay the Fear

Take the Enneagram, MBTI, and/or Four Tendencies quiz online and spend time reading more deeply about the results and styles. Consider the implications in your own context. Are there tendencies that dominate? Which of these do you consider a signature strength? Which of these indicators do you acknowledge requires you to work your non-dominant hand in your leadership setting?

Join the conversation and share your insights on social media.
#LeadwithFAITH

CHAPTER 4

Leading with Your Signature Strengths

The snow is only meant, created, commanded to fall. The rain is only meant, created, commanded to pour down. You were only meant, created, commanded to be who you are, weird and wonderful, imperfect and messy and lovely.

—*Shauna Niequist*, Present Over Perfect

G***rowth mindset***, a term often used in the education field and attributed to Carol Dweck, has strong application for our own self-discovery. From her body of thirty years of research, the most basic discovery posits people's underlying beliefs about their abilities make up either a fixed or a growth mindset. In a fixed mindset, a person believes there is a limit to what they can learn based upon makeup, condition, etc. A growth mindset proposes a person can overcome challenges, fail, learn, and keep growing in their thinking. Though that description is as far as I will dive in this text, I acknowledge determining your own mindset, whether growth or fixed, may help to remove your own barriers to personal development you may encounter as you read through these sections. Dweck's website, Mindworks, has a solid tool for assessing your own mindset on growth, and you can find that link in the resources section. For now, I will continue on with the assumption that we are all working toward a growth mindset. Implication otherwise would mean that you do not intend to grow your own courageous leadership skills, and this book would be a colossal waste of your time.

We all possess areas of strength and room for growth in a wide range of spaces, from content skill sets to critical thinking to behavior tendencies. If we approach life from a growth mindset, we believe that all beings have the ability to learn, to develop, to change their way of thinking, and to learn new skills throughout their lifetime. Just ask this lady about learning how to record, edit, and produce a podcast whether or not we can learn something new! The *In AWE Podcast* that I host weekly would never have taken off had I not been willing to learn and grow new skills and knowledge. Stories from amazing women would not reach the hearts of those who listen every week had I not discovered how to embrace and use my strengths in that space either!

Important to note here is that we can sometimes be our worst critic and the one who holds us back the most from becoming our best version. It is too easy to hold self-limiting beliefs and have those play on the reel of our minds on repeat to the point where we believe them. We all face overcoming "impostor syndrome," where these self-limiting beliefs become pervasive and create an interior monologue known as the inner critic. For me, that critic played heavily in the early months of launching out of school leadership, and the constant chatter threatened to sink me. "I am not an entrepreneur and have always worked for someone else. There is no way I can make enough money for my family doing this work. Without the title of principal, I have no credibility in leadership. The technology is too complicated. I don't have enough social media presence or influence." How did I beat that back?

I identify that voice as the ultimate impostor, Satan truly, and if I listen to those lies, then I am not believing the true identity I have as a daughter of Christ. I cannot claim that the fears don't spike or poke through the barrier I place, but I can tell you that identifying the criticism in that way allows me to kick it back hard. In fact, in a seeking stage of learning, growing, and questioning, a person may feel only other people can label their work as valuable. Without hesitation, I confidently counter that the world is not who gives me authority. I am who my Heavenly Father says I am; therefore, I battle back that ugly impostor with affirmation and a reminder that where I place my identity matters a great deal.

With that, the inner monologue shifts: *You know what, Sarah? You are correct that you do not yet know how to be an entrepreneur. But you do have leadership skills, ability to see beauty in this world, internal drive, passion for the messages you want to share, love for others, desire to amplify others' stories, and decent interviewing skills. Turns out you can learn to podcast. Oh, you do not know how to build a website? Okay, then ask some people. Pay another person to do the really hard stuff and continue to grow your learning while you keep moving forward, one step at a time. Just keep taking those steps forward.*

This is the way we lead from our signature strengths. Yes, we can grow and we should, but harnessing where we are strong allows us to battle the inner critic and embrace what makes us awesome at something versus sitting in perceived failure before we even begin! If we listen too much to the inner critic about what we cannot do well, we forget about the ways we are strong. Your unique strengths are what empower you to lead boldly instead of meekly in fear.

> Your unique strengths are what empower you to lead boldly.

FAITH IN ACTION
LAVONNA ROTH, AUTHOR, SPEAKER, CONSULTANT FOR IGNITE YOUR S.H.I.N.E.®

Am I good enough? This question drove me for years and still haunts me at times in the darker crevices of my thoughts. What I've come to discover is that I am not alone in this fear. It's a fear of not measuring up. A fear of not being as good at something as someone else. A fear of disappointment. This list could go on, and it is different for each of us and may be different at different times in our life.

But that's just it . . . it's a fear. Having the fear of not being good enough led me to the unattainable goal of perfectionism and to people pleasing. I lived my life for everyone else and for what I thought everyone wanted—everyone but me.

My life-changing moment came when I was in a major car accident. I hydroplaned on the highway, crashing into the trees in the median, and I was later told by highway patrol that they thought no one survived. That accident resulted in me taking a hard look at myself and my life. Why wasn't my life taken? I do not have an answer for that, but what I can answer is that I am so grateful it was not. That moment, that horrific moment, changed me. It made me realize that I was here for a reason! We all get one life. Just one. So how we choose to live it is up to us. Again, how we choose to live it is up to us.

You get to make the choice. Yes, you. You can rattle off every excuse in the book as to why you can't, but what if you could? What if you had to? What if by doing so, you got to experience the freedom of being the beautiful you and the life you want to lead? What if by doing so you impacted others even more by sharing the value you have? *Ahhhh* . . . relief. Plus, you are giving a gift to so many others in return. When you choose not to share your value, on the other hand, you rob others of an opportunity to be better by what you offer.

I strongly believe we are all truly exceptional and beautiful in our own way. Despite that truth, our brains automatically look for the negative, then we learn through society to compare ourselves. This is a cycle we must break! Imagine if we took a step back and viewed ourselves through the eyes of a loving friend. This may be difficult to do because of our past, the stories we create, and the imperfections we allow to trouble us; however, when we tear down the words that have been said to us and strip away the beliefs formed from those words or thoughts, we experience true freedom. The freedom to fly. The freedom to be exceptional. The freedom to be who we were meant to be.

Here's what I know and believe: We can let our fears own us, or we can own them. We get to choose.

+++

It is important to note a few things about exercising our signature strengths. One is that we need to spend real time identifying them, as well as understanding that we all come into this place with varying degrees of confidence and self-doubt. In working with students as a building leader, one of my favorite experiences was a yearly youth retreat our guidance counselor organized through a company called Youth Frontiers. One of their key lessons was honoring yourself. They highlighted a story about taking a math test and receiving a 97 percent. That's a great score! However, our brains are wired too easily to focus on the three that we got wrong. Our brains often scan for the negative in the world, and, according to Shawn Achor, a well-known researcher in the area of positive psychology and author of *The Happiness Advantage*, "Constantly scanning the world for the negative comes with a great cost. It undercuts our creativity, raises our stress levels, and lowers our motivation and ability to accomplish goals." We need to train our minds and put into action a focus on the positive aspects around us, including our own positive attributes. When you move into the space of identifying and *exercising* your signature strength, train your focus on the strengths first.

As with any muscle, our strengths get stronger when we regularly practice and exercise them. We need to be intentional. You don't build muscle and tone by stopping and starting a strength training regimen. You need to be consistent and, over time, the growth comes.

So, let's talk signature strengths. Too often we do an assessment of our skills and then focus on the areas of growth to improve. This makes sense in certain aspects of our lives, and, conventionally, we want to develop in our weak areas. For this section, however, it is important that we look at leading to our strengths and growing them to our highest ability. What are you already good at that you could become epic at? To frame this, let's look at the VIA Institute's work on signature strengths because they have the research and the vetted tools to back it up. In this section, we are talking about character strengths, which impact us as people and leaders in every space of our lives.

A helpful resource for this work of discovering and leading from our strength comes from the VIA Institute on Character, a nonprofit research center whose mission is to "help people change their lives by tapping into the power of their own greatest strengths." According to their research, twenty-four character strengths are universal to us all. You can find them in the table below for review, but I caution you to not start self-identifying on your own. It is too easy to come into any self-assessment with blinders and move too quickly. I urge you to engage with the assessment at the end of this section in a way that will have an impact on you moving forward in your leadership. When you choose to engage with the free assessment, you will be able to identify your own signature character strengths.

In the table on the following pages, Dr. Ryan Niemiec of the VIA Institute on Character illustrates the summary of the organization's research findings. Each of the twenty-four traits from the study—as well as a brief description and frequency with which those who participated in the study identified as their top five strengths—appear in the chart below. Launching into our best selves through our five strongest traits empowers our journey, and they universally apply within any context of our lives.

Positive psychology research on this topic of signature strengths continues to grow, and whole books have been written around the traits. I am just devoting a chapter here in this book, so consider how you might want to look into this more deeply for your own leadership. For now, however, understand that leading as your most authentic, free-to-be-you self will involve you exercising those signature strengths. This means you won't just take the inventory, check the box, and wear the strengths as a badge. While you may want to make a nice word collage and post it on the #LeadwithFaith hashtag, I encourage you do more than declare your strengths. Take the next steps and begin exercising these strengths daily. Work those muscles!

CHARACTER STRENGTH	SNAPSHOT VIEW	FREQUENCY IN TOP 5
Creativity	Originality that is useful	25%
Curiosity	Exploration/novelty seeking	34%
Judgment	Critical thinking and rationality	33%
Love of Learning	Systematic deepening of knowledge	28%
Perspective	The wider view	13%
Bravery	Facing fears, overcoming adversity	14%
Perseverance	Keep going, overcome all obstacles	17%
Honesty	Being authentic	31%
Zest	Enthusiasm for life	9%
Love	Genuine, reciprocal warmth	33%
Kindness	Doing for others, compassion	32%
Social Intelligence	Tune in, then savvy; insight into what makes others tick	15%
Teamwork	Collaborative, participating in group effort	15%

Fairness	Equal opportunity for all	35%
Leadership	Positively influencing others	14%
Forgiveness	Letting go of hurt, showing mercy	17%
Humility	Achievement does not elevate worth	9%
Prudence	Wise caution	9%
Self-Regulation	Self-management of vices	4%
Appreciation of Beauty and Excellence	Seeing the life behind things	25%
Gratitude	Thankfulness	29%
Hope	Positive expectations/ goals	14%
Humor	Offering pleasure/ laughter	27%
Spirituality	Connecting with the sacred	19%

Part of the research about signature strengths includes identifying and deploying your top five into your home and workspace. Work environments where leaders and employees intentionally exercise up to four signature strengths per day are more positive, achieve higher, and demonstrate stronger satisfaction, according to Dr. Ryan Niemiec.

Not surprising to my social media followers is that one of my top signature strengths resulted as appreciation of beauty and excellence, which means I am able to see the beauty around me (hello, overpost of sunrises) and appreciate work in excellence. I am in awe of things that others may take for granted. I admire great art and science, such as what may be seen in music, movies, and drama, and jobs done to high standards. Now, that would be easy to file away, simply acknowledging the strength as something I already do well. Yet there are some days when I do not capture a picture of the sun or write down the moments that inspire me. Days without those elements present as dreary and less positive. And guess what? Those were the days when I was trying to dampen this strength because it made others uncomfortable. Forget that, people! We need to be ourselves, and when we lead from a place of fear or feelings of unworthiness, the result is we become miserable, and so do those around us because we are not leading with our greatest capacity and energy. I now use this strength to encourage others by amplifying what makes humans beautiful and excellent every week on the *In AWE Podcast*.

How in the world could I exercise this seemingly useless signature strength in the world of school leadership? Appreciating beauty and excellence seems soft. Intangible. That is, until you start applying it to those around you and taking the strength of truly seeing those images in action. A lifelong goal of mine has been to speak the honor out loud when I am thinking a compliment about others instead of keeping those positive thoughts to myself and moving on without mention. Turns out my signature strength has been with me all along, and I had no idea it was a strength because when I was young, I just thought all people were inspired by the sound of drainage water flowing from the fields into the sewer system as a miraculous moment because of the background of the birds chirping. No joke, I wrote a poem about it on spiral bound notebook when I was a kid: "The Babbling Brook." My sister can verify. And just this morning (and yesterday morning), I heard the same sound isolated and amplified as I ran out in the morning cold where the silence of the world allowed the strings of the rivulets flowing together along the grass and into the drain added a beautiful ribbony flow to the cadence of my footfalls. Friends, I had no idea this was a strength! So how do I exercise this strength in character as a leader?

- During a staff meeting, when the sun would shine so brightly through the windows that it could be distracting and annoying, I would pause. Close my eyes. Take a breath in the beauty and sometimes mention it. Such a simple gesture would center me through a lot of tension-filled days but would also allow for my staff to breathe too. Some appreciated that. Some just continued to be annoyed. But exercising that strength influenced a few. And then they influenced others throughout the day.

- Noticing excellence in work is one thing, but placing this strength into action means verbalizing or acknowledging in some way with honor. I made it my intention to both publicly and privately (depending upon the staff members' preferences, which took both time and intention to learn) honor their work on projects. One of my favorites was nominating my agriculture teacher for an award and her getting it! Notice excellence. Put it into action.

- I stand in awe of the way people and stories are connected. Putting this strength into action meant noticing and sometimes acknowledging it in the moment and being willing to say what others wouldn't. When working with people, seeing the beauty for them is a strength. I would point out the positives and allow affirmations to seep in, relishing the moment they could see the beauty too. It is also an honor to do this with my children every day.

- My daughters now look at the sky and thank God for the beautiful painting because they have seen me do it hundreds of times. Influencing others to see beauty matters.
- Exercising this strength means being intentional about handwritten notes that provide specific acknowledgement of excellence, not a simple thank you. I am good at that!

In my early years of leadership, I led completely as myself. In awe of it all. Though it was a bit much for people to take all the time, I was my happiest in my work environment. My energy flowed, and I faced down a lot of fears. Unfortunately, when I transitioned into a new space, I began to dial back the character strengths that truly made me *me*. During a time of disruption, I was told my smile seemed fake, there was no way I could be so joyful, and that it wasn't right to be happy amidst everyone else's sadness.

Readers, this after I had endured the near demise of my marriage, the loss of a brother from suicide, and countless trials at home and work.

Too happy.

When I began adjusting the tone of my leadership to the demands of those around me based on their perceived needs, we all lost. There are some who would accuse me of being fake for a few years. They are right to a degree. When I was leading out of fear in that time, not exercising my signature strengths enough, not feeling free to really be me and to lead from my strengths, fear took over. And though it certainly was not all bad, I look at that chapter of a few months as staining. Damaging.

I also know now what I didn't know then. A person with a joyful disposition certainly does not feel happy all the time. So when the person accused me of being fake, the story I started to tell myself was that they must be right. After all, I was always smiling, always trying to bring joy to others, but feeling intense sadness at times. That must have made me a hypocrite, right? Wrong! Through Brené Brown's work, I have recently been given the gift of clarity in this space. Happiness is to organizational climate what joy is to culture. Happiness is a feeling based upon a set of circumstances. You bet it was hard to be happy when it felt like I was being challenged in all aspects of life, losing a lot of stability, and facing a lot of negativity! But joy is a state of being and a commitment to find the rhythm to the beat of the waves with a smile on your face, even in the raging seas of life.

Exercise your signature strengths with gusto and lead with faith, my friends. I will never fall into that trap again. Ever. If I am to lead in another organization, it will be with FAITH in all aspects or not at all. We cannot be authentic and dampen our strengths. We must lead from our strengths.

> *We cannot be authentic and dampen our strengths.*

I don't want to leave this topic without stating that my example is not simple. I understand that leading with emotional intelligence is key, and we will delve into that in the section on Heart. At no time did I believe that my leadership was ever tone deaf and naive to diminish people's sadness. Another strength of mine is being able to gauge the emotional climate of a space. When a person tells me I am too happy as a joyful Enneagram seven, my response will forever and always be that I am a thermostat, not a thermometer. It is my job to set the tone as a leader of any organization. To acknowledge the grief and pain of others with compassion is completely different from falling into the pit alongside them. As leaders, we need to be sensitive to others' needs, of course. We must also ensure that adapting our behaviors in a moment does not mean that we dampen ourselves and our light in the process.

Once you have determined your own signature strength, it is absolutely key to create a plan to be intentional about exercising it every day.

In my new space, I keep notes on my phone to document the beauty and excellence around me. I send notes in the mail twice a week to acknowledge people, both in my professional and personal circles. I post gorgeous pictures on my social media accounts to inspire others. And I verbalize when I notice beauty and excellence so I can speak the honor into the world and my children can be influenced by this strength.

What will you do with yours? Remember, daily exercise.

Building upon Weakness

Please notice how small this section is in relation to that of exercising your strengths. Leading with faith does not mean you ignore the areas that need more fruit to be produced. It means that you celebrate the way you were made and ignite the brightest light from that space. This is not a license to ignore areas upon which you can grow. We all want to become better. Just don't dwell on the negative and the fear pit in the space you need to grow. Focus on the fruit of your spirit first. Seriously, if you have not done that yet, skip this section and come back.

Now, if you have analyzed your character strengths and created a plan to exercise daily from your top five, then consider selecting one to work on to strengthen. We are working on a lot in this text, and overextending can burn us out. If you are going to focus on character development, your greatest gains will come from practicing your strengths. When you select an area of growth, consider a few things. In reality, if you take the character strength in which you are weakest, of course you will see growth. But it may take *a lot of energy*. And you have to decide if you are up to that challenge just now, or if growth in that area is better as a long-term goal.

Having said that, if self-regulation is a weakness for you, as it is for the majority of the population taking the VIA Institute survey, and vices are harming you or those around you, this may be the jolt you needed to get started. Remember, just like with exercising our strengths, daily small doses of growth are key.

If you are going to focus on character development, your greatest gains will come from practicing your strengths.

If we follow the exercise analogy, consider that sometimes in the reaching, you can pull a muscle that stops all progress. If you are so uncomfortable with one of the character traits that it is painful to reach for, select one you know you can grow well. Now, this is not research based. This is Sarah Faith.

When we look back at the chart on pages 40–41, we see that self-regulation—management of vices—represents four percent of the population's top five. Man, if you struggle with that one, you are not alone. None of us have that one figured out completely, and in our world of instant gratification, temptations increase in challenge to overcome. This one, however, might be the key to everything for you in leadership, both in life and home. If you are struggling with vices, leading with faith over fear means you don't ignore them just because positive psychology tells you to focus on what you can grow. You and I need to be stronger than that.

Major vulnerability time for me, friends. Vices. Once I met my husband at the age of nineteen, I stopped drinking alcohol. Yes, process that one. He was so viscerally against it, and I was so quickly smitten, that giving it up, as well as any lifestyle tied to it, was so easy. I said for years that I started all my good habits when I met him. And I am thankful for that gift so I could be focused; I know my trajectory for success was directly tied to this habit.

Enter the 2014–2015 school year, and the truth is, that changed. I was introduced to wine. No big deal. A glass or two. I found out that I liked Riesling, but I really loved Moscato. And without belaboring this point, over the course of four years, I began to love it enough that I not only bought it by the case, but friends and family would gift it to me. I received wine glasses for Christmas, and a glass turned into two, which morphed into three most nights of the week. Now, in working at exercising my character strengths (deficit), I would give it up occasionally. Months at a time, I would go dry to prove to myself and others that I could go without it. Red flag. Alcoholism can be a family trait. Even those of us with alcoholism in our family tree can have alcohol every now and then to no ill effect, but my patterns began to prove that I am not one of those people and that my family history was going to work against me in this case.

As part of my goals for 2019, I was given #SLAY as my #OneWord. With that focus came some directives from the Holy Spirit and some guidelines. This was a directive. No alcohol for 2019. Astonishingly, that has not been hard for me. Sure, I make jokes about it and have longed for it at social gatherings (a class reunion) or some nights to relax, but cutting it cold has not been a problem for the entire year. It doesn't mean that other vices haven't taken over, i.e., more chocolate, gum, coffee, social media.

I have a long way to go in vice defeating, but I hope my acknowledgment of a battle here will help you with your own. There is a reason four percent of the population lists self-regulation as a strength, but we can work on it so it is not a weakness that creates a fall into the pit of fear.

Okay, that was an intense example, so let me give you a more palatable daily example in leadership. One thing I'm known for is having treats on the ready for staff and visitors to my office. I always love having candy, particularly chocolate. This was awesome for creating a welcoming environment and bringing joy to people. Staff members' kids would always come to my office after school and know where to get the supply, allowing me to have informal and relationship-building chats. When law enforcement had to come in for any reason, it was nice to boost them with a bit of their favorite treat. But I can see how my own lack of self-regulation in that space was detrimental for those I led who were trying to fight their own battle. Some had to avoid the sugar for health reasons. Let's be honest: We all need to avoid it for those reasons! Simple moves like bringing apples to leadership team meetings helped both my team and I with this, but there were some who still wanted the chocolate. I tried to do both.

Face the Fear

Was there anything in this chapter that worried you or had you feeling inadequate or uncomfortable? Name it now so you can explore your strengths further. In reviewing the character strengths, are there any that lend themselves to your own context better than others? When you read the section about focusing on strengths rather than weaknesses, what was your reaction and how can you apply this concept to your work?

Slay the Fear

Take a quiz, identify your signature strengths, and develop a plan for exercising daily those strengths.

Join the conversation and share your insights on social media.
#LeadwithFAITH

GATHERING STONES
RESOURCES FOR FURTHER EXPLORATION

- **Chris Heuertz's Blog (Enneagram)**: chrisheuertz.com/enneagramreadinglist
- **RHETI inventory through the Enneagram Institute**: enneagraminstitute.com
- **Wegner-Enneagram Personality Style Scales**: wepss.com
- *For the Love Podcast* **with Jen Hatmaker, Episode 2 with Chris Heuertz**: jenhatmaker.com/episode-02-enneagram.htm; there are a ton of resources in that episode to engage with further.
- **MBTIBasics**: myersbriggs.org/my-mbti-personality-type/mbti-basics
- **The Four Tendencies Quiz**: quiz.gretchenrubin.com
- **VIA Institute on Character Survey**: viacharacter.org/character-strengths

SECTION TWO
Purpose in Leadership Affirmed

You are good at something for a reason. God designed you this way, on purpose. It isn't fake or a fluke or small. These are the mind and heart and hands and voice you've been given, so use them.

—Jen Hatmaker

Affirmed in Purpose Foundations

- We lead more consistently and less out of fear when we identify and operate out of our core values.
- Affirmed in purpose means we have the sanctuary of core beliefs to lean into when the world is trying to lead us elsewhere.
- Defining our personal mission guides us in our actions today to align our steps toward the vision of the version we will be in the future.

n December 4, 2006, just months before I completed my degree in educational administration, I wrote the following words in a notebook:

> *There are times when I am so unhappy I question every situation in which I find myself. Why am I a teacher? Why do I try so hard? Why bother trying to please everyone? The thankless nature of my career is already getting to me, not even three years into it. There is a real disconnect in my burnout status and my desire to be a principal who never wants teachers to reach that status. Daunting. At what point do you stop giving? Do kids care, notice, understand? At this point, it feels simply like they could care less if you are there and certainly aren't thankful, but expectant. Do they care? Do I impact their decisions? I am sure one day I'll get some type of sign for what I am doing. Is there more? Do I improve people's lives? I think of Katherine Lane. Do my discussions help or hinder her? Sometimes I can't tell. I have so much respect for her and for who she has the potential of becoming. Do I matter to her? Why can't I sit here and enjoy my evening instead of thinking about kids—it's a way of life.*

At that time in my life as I do again now, I processed and reflected often in journals. I was an English teacher, after all, and a lifelong reflective writer. In this post, interestingly enough, I mention getting a sign someday, and I did. What follows is the account of that sign, and I hope it blows your mind open because retyping it has my heart pounding in awe of its significance.

On April 9, 2015, I was rooting around for a notebook for my daughter who was insisting she needed one for school. In April. In full disclosure, I am not the neatest organizer. Okay, I am a full-out mess, but I usually know where items hang out in my house and my office. I knew I had some spiral bound notebooks in the drawer of the trusty old desk in my bedroom. Though I had endured a long, stressful day at school (let's be honest . . . it was more like a long, stressful year), I was determined to help my daughter with this task and focus on her and not my own stress. I found a few notebooks, which I instantly recognized. One would have multiple entries in it from my days of teaching journaling in the classroom and modeling the behavior. The other was a left-behind notebook I had kept and brought home—because who wastes valuable paper? *Ta-da!* That would be the one. We had already endured one meltdown from me presenting a less-than-perfect notebook to my six-year-old, so I opened it up to be sure it was empty. There was one entry in it. Dated December 4, 2006. I stopped for a moment to read it, recognizing my own handwriting. What I read weighed on my heart.

I mean, we were going through some of the worst turmoil in my district than I had ever experienced, and wisdom of hindsight tells me now, that the district had known. I felt the weight of my words and struggled with the inner critic that said, *See? Look at you, you big hypocrite. Teachers are more stressed than ever, and you are not helping them at all. Your leadership sucks. You don't belong doing this, you big poser.*

I bit back the negativity and fought back the tears that were threatening to punch through. Was I really doing this to my teachers? What a profound reflection from an early teacher! I felt gratitude that I received this reminder from myself to myself to focus on kids and help teachers do the same. We have to focus on our why.

With a renewed sense of calm, I set to getting the girls to bed. At that time, my three-year-old was not feeling well and couldn't seem to fall asleep. I was exhausted but decided to rock her to sleep. After all, I didn't get to hold her enough and certainly wasn't spending quality time with her these days, with all the extra evening meetings, paperwork, and deadlines.

As her warm breath began to slow in rhythm to the pattern of sleep, I breathed in and out. *So tired. I'll just hold her a bit longer and check up on Facebook.*

I saw a notification from a former student the second I logged in, and my heart stopped. I clicked on the message, which stated that Katherine Lane had tagged me in a post. Enter sign.

From two hours prior, at the exact moment I had read her name in the entry of my journal from nine years earlier, begging for a sign for what I am doing, the same student I mentioned responded to the following prompt from a Facebook post on a local radio station: "Who's the teacher who had the biggest influence on the person you became today?"

Katherine tagged me in her response: "My high school teacher, Sarah Johnson!! Always there for me and such a wonderful person. :)"

Mind blown. We may not always know where our influence leads. We may not always know when our messages land in this life.

Not only was the timing of this whole scenario unexplainable and needed, the content was such as well. You see, I needed to hear that what I did for Katherine mattered, but I also needed to hear that she thought it was important I was there for her. That I was a wonderful person. Because at that time on April 9, 2015, I did not feel like a wonderful person. And I also needed the reminder of how I had felt during that time when I was "always there for her." The fruits of the labor were delayed but oh-so-rich, nourishing, and perfectly timed after all.

This faithful experience reoriented and reminded me of my purpose. Though the organization I was in at the time appeared not to value relationships, and building them was a struggle I had not faced to that point, I was reminded that my core value has always been for the kids and for people, helping others. This sign was a perfect reminder that my influence mattered. Our core values should always be at our forefront, but when they are not, we need reminders. This one happened to be miraculous for me.

Maybe you are in a situation where you feel ill equipped for the task or wonder why you are in that scenario. At those times in my own life in 2006 and 2015, I had not studied the story of Esther from the Old Testament. Unpacking it just a bit here reminds us that we are all given special gifts and talents we can use with great purpose. Esther exerted courage in the name of devotion to God, Mordecai, and her people. She bravely presented herself to King Xerxes using her God-given beauty and gifts to the benefit of saving her people from genocide. Esther could have enjoyed life in the palace and ignored the heavy weight of involving herself in a dangerous situation, but she rose up from her fear to slay. In Mordecai's words to Esther as she wrestled her own fear giant, we can consider our own situation for being placed in a position for "such a time as this."

> *Our core values should always be at our forefront, but when they are not, we need reminders.*

> *If you keep quiet at a time like this, deliverance and relief for the Jews will arise from some other place, but you and your relatives will die. Who knows if perhaps you were made queen for just such a time as this?*
> —Esther 4:14, NLT

Ever since I read Jen Hatmaker's book *For the Love* in which she addressed the idea that sometimes our perception of our *calling* can be a little misguided, I have honestly struggled letting that word roll off my tongue. She opened my mind to consider that a calling is easy to believe when we have certain privileges, but not really when people are born in conditions that may hinder access to freely following dreams. As Hatmaker writes, "If it isn't also true for a poor single Christian mom in Haiti, it isn't true." I do still believe that leaders are called. Our names are called, and we answer it from any space of the world in which we find ourselves. Hatmaker's broader and wiser vision helps me to keep the idea of a "calling" from being too lofty. We will dive deeper into how we can lead from any space when we talk about titles. For now, this idea of leadership as a calling is one I continue to wrestle with but cannot completely release for spiritual, personal, and professional reasons. If you are reading this book, you understand that leadership is challenging, beautiful, and simply not meant for everyone. Leadership is hard and is filled with complexities. How do you keep your eyes on your vision during the pit moments, when your self-efficacy has been shattered on the floor by a mistake or a perceived shortcoming or the inevitable disruption? We need to stay connected to our personal and professional core values as we develop and refine our mission and grow as leaders.

We need to stay connected to our personal and professional core values as we develop and refine our mission and grow as leaders.

DAVID LED AFFIRMED

Though David was just a shepherd boy and not firstborn, in fact seventh or eighth in Jesse's line depending upon which account you read, he was anointed to be king early in his life by God through Samuel. Throughout his life, David led with the firm purpose to serve and praise God in all circumstances. Whether he was felling bear and lion with the strength God gave him or a giant on the battlefield, David knew God was with him. Whether he was fleeing Saul's pursuit in the caves, worshipping the Lord in public, or gathering items for years for a temple he would never build, the work was done to glorify God and speak of God's good work in his life. David's legacy lives on today, with Jesus Christ in his lineage, all because he courageously led with purpose to worship and praise God in all circumstances.

> *I proclaim your saving acts in the great assembly;*
> *I do not seal my lips, Lord, as you know.*
> *I do not hide your righteousness in my heart;*
> *I speak of your faithfulness and your saving help.*
> *I do not conceal your love and your faithfulness from the great assembly.*
>
> —*Psalm 40: 9–10, NIV*

CHAPTER 5

Leading from Your Core Values

You don't become what you want; you become what you believe.

—Oprah Winfrey

The process for identifying core values can get complicated, but we are going to keep it simple. Very simple. And in doing that, believe me, defining them will feel like anything but simple. Living by them can be even more challenging. It is essential, however, to avoid falling prey to the false belief that we must perfectly adhere to all of our core values every day, all day long, until we die. We are simply not perfect enough to do that.

What we *can* do, however, is become aware of what matters most to us and how these values affect the way we feel and live. By keeping our core values in mind—both at home and in our professional lives—and using them as our guides, we can grow into the mature, trustworthy, and confident beings we are made to be.

When we take the time to define, communicate, and hold ourselves accountable to core values, we allow others to assist us in refining our leadership at work and at home, and that process itself builds trust, maturity, and faith. We are tested every day, tempted to fall in line with what others value or insist is important. When we live by a set of core values, overcoming these distractions is so much more attainable. Therefore, we gain in confidence in ourselves and from those we lead.

FAITH IN ACTION
JEFF KUBIAK, NORTHERN CALIFORNIA ELEMENTARY EDUCATOR, AUTHOR OF ONE DROP OF KINDNESS, ADVOCATE FOR ALL KIDS @JEFFREYKUBIAK

I never intended to be a leader, but over the years, even as a youth, I was told that I had the intuitive ability to do just so. Leading doesn't have to be charging in front of your troops to the frontlines ready to battle, nor does it need to be yelling from atop a high perch, spitting out orders to the minions.

Believe me, I've never been perfect. Never tried. I've also stumbled upon my faults, but growing up with parents that I had, overcoming obstacles—not getting "the" job, flunking a test, missing out on the top college acceptance letters, coming in second, not finding the right words—was what we did. It doesn't matter what it was or is; the Kubiaks would just find a way to redo, iterate, reflect, and lead on.

As I grew older and began to navigate the real world, I would sit back with my inner self and watch what I had done. Solid Team Member. Reliable Friend. Encouraging Father. Inspiring Coach. Selfless Teacher. Caring Spouse.

While I see all of these traits in myself, I know it hasn't been easy. The kindness. The empathy. The unconditional love. The support. These characteristics and core values have been difficult for me to find at times. Whether my navigation has been led by God, writing, listening to friends, or speaking with loved ones, I always seem to find my way back.

While I often stumble, I have always managed to find my feet, realizing that missing an Olympic team by .12 seconds, or a failed marriage, or losing my temper are all rocks to trip over in the path of life. We must remember not to let those rocks become boulders, crushing our spirit and taking away our faith in who we are.

My core values shape me. They were given to me by my parents. I, as a leader of others, must use them to help those I lead become better leaders themselves. They see my imperfections, my misdirections, and my "real" self.

As leaders, we should be transparent, honest, and show others our ability to be no one else but who we are. There is only one of you. Be you with the values you know best.

Lead with me, my friends.

+++

One of the most useful processes I have used with students as an adjunct professor for identifying core values comes from *Dare to Lead*, where Brené Brown pares the process down. What I like about the process and results is we produce actionable steps that allow us all to truly live and lead inside our values as often as possible, to act upon them intentionally, and to articulate them well so trusted allies can help us identify when we live outside of those values. (Which is often shame and fear-inducing behavior.)

Brown defines values as "a way of being or believing that we hold most important. Living into our values means that we do more than profess our values, we practice them. We walk our talk, we are clear about what we believe and hold important, and we take care that our intentions, words, thoughts, and behaviors align with those beliefs."

Core values are meant to be shared and lived by. In order to do that, we must first define them and then define the behaviors we can operate with in order to live these out. Brown encourages us to narrow our core values to two, distilling them from a list of hundreds, even though we want to select ten to fifteen. She notes that those in her research "who are most willing to rumble with their vulnerability and practice courage tethered their behavior to one or two values, not ten."

Narrowing down this list to two core values requires a lot of reflection and ability to release some values to what she calls "tier two" values, not core. My experience with this process mirrors the example she gives when she shares that not selecting family as a core value was challenging, but she realized that her actions within the core values show the commitment to family, as do mine.

My core values? Balance, resilience, and faith. Yes, I have three, and they are ordered not by importance but by the way they have rolled off my tongue for months. When I consider these core values, an illustration of living in them was the day I had to turn down a dream contract recently. The organizer had sought me out through my website, and the work was in one of my favorite states, during my favorite time of year, with a crew of principals! It would pay well, and I had literally just been praying over booking a speaking engagement for November. My heart sunk as I checked flights and realized there was no possible way to accept this contract and be with my kids and husband for Halloween.

To understand this dilemma, let me back up. When we were searching for our first house way back in 2004, we visited many in our area. As a young couple freshly married and freshly employed, we had a lot to learn about what to look for in houses. Case in point: When we saw the image on the realty site for the home in which we still live and love, my reaction to the front door was, "Joe, this is a trick-or-treating house!" And in case that is not a cute enough example, how about the fact that we were married for a full five Halloweens before we had our first daughter, and in that time I dressed up each year, going as far as purchasing a fog machine and approximately five-thousand bins of clearance Halloween décor faithfully for years. (I rose before the 5:00 a.m. hour just to drive to our nearest Walmart thirty minutes away every November 1.) Our firstborn began crawling at six months on Halloween toward her favorite book, *Trick or Treat Countdown*. In recent years, my husband began a tradition where he "scares" us and comes to the door with a toddler pumpkin costume on his head and the girls still don't know when he is coming. In 2016, when I ran the Marine Corps Marathon on October 30, I vowed that it would not interfere with Halloween, which meant a series of events which led to me not even eating my first meal until four hours after coming across the line, making it to the airport barely showered but on time. My sister had traveled with me, and her presence kept me going, as did the best tasting buffalo wings and margarita I ever had, until we met my parents. They took over for the two-and-a-half-hour leg to my hometown, allowing me to sleep in a coma-like state until we got home, and I woke in my bed safely to Halloween with my then seven- and five-year-olds, ready to enjoy their giddy spirits in time for the holiday. When it comes to Halloween, we don't play around.

Though I wanted so badly for it all to work out with this contract, there was no puzzle that could work, no flight that would take off in the middle of the night or even late enough to allow me an hour with my family. No compromise.

And so I turned it down. As painful as it was to say no to an opportunity to impact lives with my balance message and provide for my family my portion of our expenses for the month, I could not let go of one of the few remaining experiences of my daughters' childhoods on that sugar-filled, family-saturated evening.

If I am to live in my values—balance, resilience, faith—this "no" moment exemplified doing so. Satisfying balance in my life always prioritizes family, resilience always presses me to bounce through challenge, in this case financial, and faith tells me that when I follow what is in line with my greater purpose, we are most blessed. I shared with the organizer my reasons for not being able, stating that I wouldn't be living in my values if I took this work, then shared contact information for my colleague. The organizer indicated she would love to offer another date and that my example was exactly what they were looking for in the balance message I would bring.

Living in our values is not always easy. But it is always right.

Affirming your core values starts with defining them. Keep in mind you are looking to identify your core values, isolating a few essential concepts from a list of potentially hundreds. To keep things simple, I have listed just fifty potential values. You can add to this list if you'd like. Review the list and then use one (or both) of the processes that follow to more clearly define your core values. I have used both of these processes, and each has served its purpose at different stages of my leadership journey. Feel free to select the process that works best for you currently.

Option 1: The *Dare to Lead* Method for Identifying Your Core Values

1. From the list on the next page, circle the fifteen values that resonate most with you.

Which of These Values Most Resonate with You?

Authenticity	Family	Peace
Achievement	Friendship	Pleasure
Adventure	Fun	Poise
Authority	Growth	Popularity
Autonomy	Happiness	Recognition
Balance	Honesty	Reputation
Beauty	Humor	Resilience
Boldness	Influence	Respect
Compassion	Inner Harmony	Responsibility
Challenge	Justice	Security
Citizenship	Kindness	Self-respect
Community	Knowledge	Service
Competency	Leadership	Spirituality
Contribution	Learning	Stability
Creativity	Love	Success
Curiosity	Loyalty	Status
Determination	Meaningful Work	Trustworthiness
Fairness	Openness	Wealth
Faith	Optimism	Wisdom

2. Sit with those values for as long as you need to and narrow down your list to only two. As you think about each word, ask yourself the following questions:
- Does this define me?
- Is this who I am at my best?
- Is this a filter that I use to make hard decisions?

3. Define the behaviors aligned with the values. (Repeat for each value.)

Value: _____
- What are three behaviors that support your value?
- What are three slippery behaviors that are outside your value?
- What's an example of a time when you were fully living in this value?

While there is more work we can all do around this topic of building core values at work and with a team, our purpose seeks to narrow and define behaviors as a start for your foundation. For readers who would like to dive further into this process, find more in the Gathering Stones section.

Option 2: Develop Five to Ten Personal Core Values

Another more open-ended process by Iowa City School District Superintendent Stephen Murley prompts you to think deeply about the values, answer a series of questions, and yields a lengthier list. I once engaged in this very process and shared with my staff at the start of a year.

Consider a meaningful moment or positive moment that stands out:
- What was happening to you?

- What was going on?
- What values were you honoring then?

Consider a negative moment that stands out:
- What was happening to you?
- What was going on?
- What were you feeling?
- What values were being suppressed?

What is most important in your life?
- Beyond your basic human needs, what must you have in your life to experience fulfillment?
- What are the personal values you must honor or a part of you withers?

Identify each value that is essential to you.
- Group the values you've identified into related themes.
- Select a word that best represents the group.

Analyze the groups.
- What values are essential to your life?
- What values represent your primary way of being?
- What values are essential to supporting your inner self?

Distill the list to five to ten personal core values.
- Rank the list in order of importance.

Analyze the final list.
- How does reading the list of values you've identified make you feel?
- Do you feel they are consistent with who you are?
- Are they personal to you?
- Do you see any values that feel inconsistent with your identity, as if they belong to someone else, like an

authority figure or society, and not you?
- Check your priority ranking— do you feel like your values are in the proper order of importance?

After you have defined your core values, share them with your team, your family, your friends. Communicating your core with your stakeholders allows the opportunity to clarify and build trust. Invite your team to gracefully question you when they think that you may be acting outside of these values. While your core values are not everyone's, they are yours. They define who you are. Communicating them and referring back to them as a filter for actions, can clear a path in the clutter of life.

Invite your team to gracefully question you when they think that you may be acting outside of your core values.

Getting to the Core: A Steppingstone to the Leap of Faith

It was not until the start of my fourth year in the organization I most recently led that I defined and shared my core values. After experiencing a tumultuous three years, I realized that those I led did not know who I was as a person clearly, even in the face of daily action and continued commitment to them and experiencing exceptional challenge in that role. In that space, I learned, probably the hard way, that people only see shards of light, even when we are pouring it out in beams. In an effort to grow, I had been taking coursework for superintendency, and one of the exercises was to define core values. I shared them with staff at our initial meeting that year. At that point, I realized I had been intentionally trying to lead from behind for so long due to all the turmoil that I had failed to step out front and take hold of the space. It is one thing to define a mission and vision with values for a school, but if you don't do this as an individual and share that with the people you lead, how will they know you are authentic? That is not easy. It is vulnerable. And faithful. Brave. Courageous. Necessary. Consider the powerful connection we can build when we lead that way.

I don't think it was a coincidence that after I had defined and planned to share my own core values, the leader that came into town as our superintendent (my third in that district in four years) did the same thing. He sat all building leaders down individually to share his ten core values as a leader, and we had a discussion about it. Being on the receiving end of this practice was not only refreshing and trust building, it gave me an opportunity to size up our ideologies in relation to our leadership work. When the leader in charge of the organization shares where they stand on the big issues, you will always know if you'll be able to stand together on them or not, and that matters a lot in leadership.

When faced with a challenge that year in my leadership, I went back to his core values and to mine. We were able to charge forward together on an initiative that ended up not having the support of the teachers, a faction of the community, or the board. But we knew that our faithful leadership together in this mattered. We were able to respect one another, respect the work, and though the decision and work did not go the way we wanted, we knew we were leading inside our core values—together. That was powerful. It allowed me to keep moving through the fear of public perception, hard conversations, and the ultimate demise of a plan that represented a lot of work and energy from many staff members. Knowing that I was operating out of my core values, it didn't flatten my spirit for that to happen. Although I may have stepped a little differently if I could again, my actions were always tied to core values. And I can sleep well because of that, even if a crew of people didn't like me for it.

I see now how living out of my core, communicating it bravely to staff, and choosing to live by those values fortified my strength as a faithful leader. Clearly, this served as an initial footfall to allow me to courageously take a giant leap.

Face the Fear

Defining core values can be a challenging exercise. Do you have any stumbling blocks in your way for defining them? Have you done this before? Are they still holding true in your life? Do you fear sharing them with others in your organization, and, if so, why might that be?

Spend time reviewing the core values exercises and decide which process you think would be most helpful to yield results. Decide on a maximum number you will define.

Slay the Fear

Develop your core values utilizing Brené Brown's or Stephen Murley's process and share them out with the #LeadwithFaith hashtag.

Join the conversation and share your insights on social media.
#LeadwithFAITH

CHAPTER 6

Determine Your Mission and Vision

If you have a vision, then you also have the power to make it happen.

—Jon Gordon

*I*n the education field, we hear a lot of great messaging about remembering our why when it comes to our work. Many could distill that down to one word: students. I am most certain that the impetus for most educators getting into their varied positions is to serve students. Yet I believe it really has to run deeper than that. When you peel apart the complex layers associated with being an educator in any role, we know that what is best for students should certainly be our filter, and we see much of what we do through that lens; however, with the varied pressures that start to build priorities in any school setting, we can see how easily that original vision can get cloudy. Add to it the fact that we may have only a slice of students in mind when we are focusing them as our why. We need to be intentional about determining a clear mission we can accomplish in our roles and just as intentional about *living* by that mission. Just like living within our values empowers us to lead with courage and forge through fires when we know it's right, living and acting in a way that aligns with our mission carries a powerful punch in the face of all the distractions that hit us while leading an organization. And to be clear, if you don't know what your own mission in life and in work is, how are you going to know how you can best lead in the organization in which you are employed?

Consider this: If you do not define your vision and mission, you will not know if the organization in which you function is the best place for you to lead. Just as knowing your own strengths, personality type, and motivations is critical to functioning in leadership, the self-awareness that comes with defining your vision and mission is critical to your ability to be the steady ship in the inevitable stormy seas of life.

> *The self-awareness that comes with defining your vision and mission is critical to your ability to be the steady ship in the inevitable stormy seas of life.*

FAITH IN ACTION
JENNIFER HOGAN, 2018 ALABAMA ASSISTANT PRINCIPAL OF THE YEAR HOOVER, ALABAMA @JENNIFER_HOGAN

I'm lucky. There's not a day that goes by when I have uncertainty about my role as an educator. But it hasn't always been that way. When I was a young teacher, I would ask myself often, "Is being an educator what I'm supposed to be doing with my life?" After teaching for four years, I quit teaching and ran a business with my husband. It was during that time away from education where I realized that being an educator was what I was supposed to be doing.

Fast forward six years from when I returned to education, and I became a high school assistant principal. Then three years later, I accepted a job as a principal in a nearby district. During my time in that district, I realized that my beliefs, morals, and practices did not align with the district leadership, so I pivoted and took a position as a teacher in a different school and district. I taught for two years before moving into an assistant principal role, where I currently continue to serve many years later.

Moving from the position of principal to teacher was a step made on faith. I personally struggled with the idea of leaving the principalship and the imposter syndrome showed up in full force. I worried that others would question my abilities and doubt if I could fulfill the role of a principal again. I had to keep believing that God would help me find purpose and face my personal demons, all while I was struggling financially to make ends meet for my family after moving from a principal's salary to a teacher salary.

During my second year in the classroom, God showed up big. One day I noticed that one of my quiet students was upset. After that class period, we had advisory in my room. The student approached my desk and asked if I had time for him. When he came around my desk, he sat on the floor and started crying. I handed him a notepad and asked him to write down what was going on with him. He wrote that he had a loaded gun in his backpack and that he had planned to kill himself that morning. After getting our intervention counselor and school resource officers to the room to assist the student, I prayed for the student and thanked God for putting me in his path.

There is not a day I take for granted when it comes to making time for a student or trying to build a connection because I have faith stronger than ever that God has put them in my path for a reason. Every interaction has purpose, is important, and is one we can't take for granted.

A Vision of What Could Be

If a mission statement is what you are today and how your actions can be informed in the now, a vision statement is one that provides a place to which you will aspire to achieve. Too often, we lump values, mission, and vision together as if they are interchangeable entities, and I have been guilty of this. Hopefully moving through these brief exercises will assist you in bringing the distinction to the table for your own organization when you consider the nuances. People and organizations who do this process well create a space for individuals to align with the collective mission and work toward a shared vision.

Your personal vision statement should be short, future oriented, definitive of who you aspire to be, and universally applicable to any role you serve in life.

Here is my vision statement:

God has called me to rise and teach masses who will see Him through the light He will continue to pour into me as I give my heart to Him first.

What I love about vision statements is they are not meant to be cast in stone, and we can refine them as we go. Seeking the clearest picture of who you want to be allows you to align your action-driven mission and set goals in all spaces to become that vision.

Who do you aspire to be? What do you want to reflect in your life? Start with the end in mind, my friends. Be brave enough to write down your vision, then commit to becoming that vision through a ceaseless and intentional strive.

Mission: Anything Is Possible

One of the best parts of attending the church that I have in the past five years is their deep commitment to a shared vision everyone can see, feel, know, and repeat. Everybody's welcome. Nobody's perfect. Anything's possible. Through the mission of existing to lead everyone to a full life in Jesus Christ, they have established core values that are clear to the church as well. I do not work in that church, yet I know the vision, mission, and values. Leadership like that is where I aspire to be, and setting a personal mission makes it possible to seek that role. Anything is possible, and creating a clear mission makes it so.

Completing a living and breathing personal mission statement will allow you to hold strong when a great idea comes your way that does not align with the statement. There are so many temptations out there, and believe me, I know this. When I left an organization to lead masses, it was challenging for me because I could do anything, follow any dream, chase down multiple pathways of success. The problem was not a lack of ideas or opportunities. The issue was not knowing my exact mission, or what I needed to do in order to get to the vision. I am still refining it in this new space, but having a personal mission allows us to align our professional mission—what a completely perfect way to live fully!

Because mission and vision often get confused, simply think of them this way:

- Your mission describes who you are today. Now. Every day. A mission takes your core values and puts them into action in a profound statement that you should be able to visibly walk out daily.
- Your vision describes what you long to be in the future. It is the guiding force for all improvement efforts and the daily actions carried out in your mission.

Your mission is who you are today.

Your vision describes what you long to be in the future.

Maya Angelou's mission has been my guiding force in some very foggy days for more than a decade. She stated, **"My mission in life is not merely to survive but to thrive and to do so with some passion, compassion, humor, and style."** This simple statement exudes so much light, wisdom, and focus. I have often used these words with students to inspire them to seek themselves among the din of teenage pressures.

You can use the same stem to draft your own mission statement: ***My mission in life is . . .***

Consider your personality traits, character strengths, and core values defined in the previous chapter, as well as actions aligned to create your own mission statement. Here is mine:

My mission in life is to utilize with excellence and intention my God-gifted passions and skills to impact others in all areas of my full life, gaining wisdom through trial and singing through triumph.

Keeping in mind a mission statement is best shared, you may choose to write one that is a shorter. Whatever the length or scope, the litmus test for a professional mission statement is whether it is something you are willing to make public so that others understand what drives you. Crafting a professional mission statement may also help you more thoroughly define your role as a leader.

Here are a few other mission statements I love. They may help you develop your own:

"To be a teacher. And to be known for inspiring my students to be more than they thought they could be."

—*Oprah Winfrey, media executive and philanthropist*

"To have fun in [my] journey through life and learn from [my] mistakes."

—*Sir Richard Branson, founder of the Virgin Group*

> **"To serve as a leader, live a balanced life, and apply ethical principles to make a significant difference."**
> —Denise Morrison, CEO of Campbell Soup Company

> **"I define personal success as being consistent to my own personal mission statement: to love God and love others."**
> —Joel Manby, CEO of Herschend Family Entertainment

> **"To use my gifts of intelligence, charisma, and serial optimism to cultivate the self-worth and net-worth of women around the world."**
> —Amanda Steinberg, founder of Dailyworth.com

When we consider ourselves as courageous leaders focused on an affirmed purpose, defining our vision and mission become critical to sustain our efforts in bold ways when we are tested. Note I didn't say if we are tested; I said when we are tested.

Face the Fear

When attempting to define a vision and a mission, are there struggles you face to put them to paper? Why might they be? Have you written one before that you might review with new eyes? Review samples of personal mission and vision statements online from a quick search. Are there any that stand out to you as particularly strong or weak? Decide if you are going to craft a personal and professional one or if you will use one for any environment.

Slay the Fear

Define your vision and mission statements, taking care to craft them in a way that infuses your values, is actionable, and can be shared. Decide where you will publish these statements so they are visible to you as a reminder of your purpose in any role.

Join the conversation and share your insights on social media.
#LeadwithFAITH

GATHERING STONES

- ***For the Love: Fighting for Grace in a World of Impossible Standards*** by Jen Hatmaker
- ***Dare to Lead: Daring Greatly and Rising Strong at Work*** by Brené Brown
- **Franklin Covey's Personal Mission Statement Builder:** msb.franklincovey.com

SECTION THREE

Intentionality to Inspire and Influence Others

Find out who you are and do it on purpose.
—Dolly Parton

Intentionality to Inspire and Influence Foundations

- We lead from priority when we set and act with intentions.
- If we are not intentional with our full lives, hours will drain away into inefficiency.
- Seeking a fuller life intentionally welcomes new possibilities and deeper tethers into our lives.
- Intentionally creating space for faith growth in our lives deepens our well.

In the darkness of the early morning, a mother rolls out of bed, exhausted from being woken several times during the dark hours, when nobody should be stirred, to assist her child who is struggling to keep her eyes closed through a variety of ailments. Last night was a sore leg. Growing pains or something worse? She makes a mental note to schedule an appointment. When was the last time her three-year-old even slept through the night? She cannot recall. Too many nights of restlessness and less than five hours of sleep to think clearly. Her last ounce of energy was sapped about five months ago from the acute grief of losing her oldest brother to suicide, and the nagging depression lingers, but she has no time to focus on that. Maybe she should take the marriage counselor up on a few solo sessions after all and figure out a better way of living.

Right now, she is living on coffee, chocolate, and adrenaline from an increasingly stressful job.

She groggily opens up her email as she presses the button to grab some jolt from the caffeine in those precious beans in liquid form. Her eyes roll over the handful of bold script names indicating unread messages that came in since the last time she checked, which had sadly been after midnight once again because there were deadlines looming heavy at work. Panic. The sub report indicates the building is short three full teacher subs for the day and a paraprofessional. Shoot. The stress rolls over her in waves, and she glances at the clock: 6:00 a.m. That leaves enough time for a quick one-mile run but not much more.

As she laces up to take the precious few minutes to herself for the day, she laments the fact that she might not even see the girls this morning, considering she has to get in early enough to ensure the building is covered. The door to her three-year-old's room opens once again, and it looks like the run will wait. After lunch supervision? No. Not during the school day. She can't even get a lunch in most days, let alone take a break for healthy exercise. People would judge that, and goodness knows there is enough public scrutiny these days. The run will probably have to wait until later, when it is dark again. But before midnight. The streak will remain.

While she lays there in the bed next to her daughter, providing some warmth and comfort, hoping it will be enough for the little one to fall back to sleep for another hour, her mind reels with all the challenges coming for the day.

Admin meeting to discuss staffing. Again. Evaluation meetings with teachers. Observations to complete since she is behind in the schedule she set before her brother died. An upset parent meeting after school. Meeting with superintendent and school attorney to review non-renewal appeal. She learned she would be basically put in front of community in an open hearing to defend the tough decision to non-renew a staff member due to budget cuts. At least the hearing got moved from the original date, her daughter's birthday. That one had nearly sent her over. Nobody had asked for her evening availability when they set the date. After all, she must be available at all times for all reasons. At least had she won that battle—barely. Then there were all the missed return calls and emails piling up, the new testing in her state, and she was responsible for teaching it districtwide with so many items to remember, and she had been spending a ton of hours learning and implementing the new system. With high-stakes accountability for all of this, the pressure was immense. They were behind on course scheduling due to the delay in staffing model, and she had been having meeting after meeting with staff members who were upset with the decisions made at the board level. Oh, shoot. And they needed to calibrate all the principals for the evaluation system, another item she was charged with leading for the district since she had previous experience—just not with this model, which literally had taken forty hours to become certified in the first place!

Her phone lights up again. Text from her superintendent. More stress.

At least her daughter is back to slumber, hopefully dreaming of the mommy who loves her enough to stay with her daddy despite the brokenness there. He had slept downstairs again last night, which was a relief. The demands of her job were too high to sit and hash out the issues now. One more stress on her burdened shoulders. She slips into the shower and out the door as the care provider shows up to replace her as the one who brushes her daughters' hair and gets them off to their day.

Friends, I wish I could tell you that any of that description was contrived. It is a shortened, amalgamated version of the reality I was living in spring of 2015. If you would have asked me at that time how I was living my legacy, I would not have wanted to answer. "Live the way in which you want to be remembered." My life quote had withered to the recesses of my former self, and the reality of my life was one I lived relentlessly persevering but struggling desperately inside. Many who knew me before this year could see a change, but I refused to show weakness on the outside. *Leaders are strong enough to handle all the things. They are able to take the hits and keep bumping along. Their feelings don't matter much, really.* That was the message I received day in and out from the state of the learning community in which I served at the time. It was not healthy for me. And honestly, it only got worse. Seriously, way worse. Student walk out. Media firestorm on campus. Lawsuits. Student death. Threats. Political turmoil. Turnover of staff: a third of the teaching staff, the entire paraprofessional staff, my lead secretary, dean of students, guidance secretary, board member turnover with shifting board presidents. And that was just the state of things at the very start of the 2015–2016 school year. There was just so much disruption, I didn't know how to be intentional about my legacy. My leadership was consistently undermined, and taking hold of my life was challenging, as my husband and I navigated seriously typhoon-like waters in our marriage.

Of course, like any time of transformation, there was growth, even if it felt slow. That subsequent year saw me taking back more of my leadership intention and reclaiming my mental health, more stability at home through hard work and more focus there, and leaning heavy into my professional relationships to grow through the turmoil. There was a shift in leadership once again, and we spent time without a superintendent, and I led through it all, my exterior remaining strong enough. My insides broken, sliced up, and bleeding.

For a period of time I wished I could just erase this whole chapter from my life. As the Holy Spirit indicated in 2018 when I needed to leave my position, I was to leave the place that "tarnished and tainted the chapters of my beautiful life." And my hand was in all of that—my inability to be intentional through the chaos, my weaknesses burgeoning and inflating every issue at home, and my lack of trust and faith in God during those years.

I can't erase that chapter, and I don't want to. I want to reflect on that time in life and gift myself with the lessons that I learned from it. I want to use it as a reminder of the type of a legacy I want to lead. Even as I muster the courage to share some of the details with you, I do so hoping that you will be that encouraged to know that it is possible to rise from the ash pit.

You can live with intention too. We can all commit to building our legacy anew. These chapters will share with you how I did it. My fervent hope is that you will take a tip or two and the strength that comes from growing your faith will carry you and help you rise. If you find yourself in the darkness of the pit, you can become strong enough to transform your life in the same way I continue to do intentionally every single day.

DAVID LED WITH INTENTIONALITY

Though there are many ways that David placed God first throughout his life, a great example that few may know is his intention with who ended up being his enemy's line. Though Saul relentlessly and viciously pursued David out of jealousy and rage for years, Saul's son Jonathan and David remained close allies. After Saul's line perished in battle, Saul ending in suicide, David treated his remains with dignity and, even more profoundly, took measures to support his friend's crippled son. Where he could have easily cast away the former king's family into exile, David lives with intention the mercy that he knows is honoring to God through showing love to his friend through this great act of service.

"Don't be afraid," David said to him, "for I will surely show you kindness for the sake of your father Jonathan. I will restore to you all the land that belonged to your grandfather Saul, and you will always eat at my table."

2 Samuel 9: 7, NIV

CHAPTER 7

Immersing Yourself in Your Full Life

The world will tell you how to live, if you let it. Don't let it. Take up your space. Raise your voice. Sing your song. This is your chance to make or remake a life that thrills you.

—Shauna Niequist, Present Over Perfect

Each one of us has a wonderfully full life with much to be grateful for and many spaces in which we should pour into the one life we were given. You are so much more than your job title and your role as a parent. What makes you tick is more than what you do for a living or the mouths you feed, the partner with whom you dance through life, or your current professional circumstances. Our lives are best carried out in every season when we are mindful of the importance of all of it, not placing so much in one area so that the other withers. I learned this the hard way, my dear readers. I mean, I didn't fail for my whole life at this. With the gift of reflection, wisdom, counsel, and awareness, I see now where I was living intentionally in so many spaces, but not all of them.

For this chapter, I want you to consider the analogy shared by Stephen Covey in *The Seven Habits of Highly Effective People*. It's also a really great lesson to reproduce for students and staff to remind us about what is important, and how we can prioritize the big rocks and fill the rest in so nothing important falls away.

As a refresher, visualize a container and a set of big rocks, a pile of pebbles, and a box of sand. If you fill the container first with sand (the least important) and pebbles and leave the big rocks for last, you will never fit your full life into that vessel. If you start with the big rocks, fill in with the pebbles, and let the sand flow in the crevices, your full life fits!

Let's be real. You cannot do all the things in every space. That is foolishness, but reducing any of the big rocks in our lives to a pebble is a fatal error. I did this with my marriage. I did this with my professional learning. Worse? I reduced my faith to the grains of sand. Seriously. For too long of a period, faith was not even in my ingredient list. And I believe wholeheartedly that is why life went astray for that time period. Without faith, I was relying on my own strength. Fatal flaw.

A blessed lesson I gained, though, is there is nothing from which we cannot be redeemed, and you can in fact take hold of your priorities. You can immerse yourself in your full life intentionally. By naming what is most important in your life and identifying ways to intentionally experience satisfaction in each of those areas each day, the rest will most certainly fall into place. It is a virtual guarantee I can provide to you. Of course, that recipe is going to be different for each of us. We also need to be willing to constantly readjust that model when changes in circumstance call for it. What feels satisfying to me now with my time in faith is very different from when I started building intentional immersion in God's word.

For this section, I am happy to reproduce for you an introduction to the framework that we provide in *Balance Like a Pirate: Going Beyond Work-Life Balance to Ignite Passion and Thrive as an Educator*, and I am going to add a section to our quadrants. I have seen the transformative power of this collectively crafted message, and though there are about a thousand other works I could reference, we also provide several in that text, so it is a great resource to head to if you are looking to grow in this particular piece of the FAITH framework.

Your full life is more than a work-life formula. There is so much more to both of these two words, so our quadrants divide our full life into four sections, and in this text, I add another.

First, the original balance quadrants:

Personal: This quadrant is about wellness in mind, body, and spirit. Within this space, we must consider mindfulness, self-care, overall health. Very importantly, this quadrant contains people, especially family and friends, but also all relationships.

Passions: In this space, the best version of us is lying dormant and waiting to be unleashed. This quadrant transcends titles from work and home and pares down to what makes us tick. Music, writing, creativity, organization, people, service, humor—name it and foster its growth.

Positional: Most often thought of as "work," this is the space where our titles live. In this quadrant, we focus upon the job title we hold and the roles and responsibilities tied to it. This quadrant is most popular among the workaholics.

Professional: This is the space in which we put forth energies to grow in our field. It is the space in our lives we make for learning and for growing our professional learning networks. In this quadrant, we are learning through coursework, reading, writing, and even presenting to other educators. This is the space where we must never stop if we are to be lifelong learners.

FAITH IN ACTION
SUZIE HENDERSON, EDD ROME, GEORGIA
@SUZIE_HENDERSON

The year I turned thirty was a year of transformation for me. I had no idea in 2005 the journey I was about to begin. What I did know, however, is that something in my life had to change. I had three small children (twin boys who were five and a daughter who was two), I was a coach's wife and a full time speech-language pathologist at our local elementary school. To say life was chaotic and busy was a gross understatement. I felt out of control and struggled each and every day with the demands of being a wife, mother, and full-time educator. I didn't feel like I was doing any one thing well.

It is at this point in my life that I learned the value and absolute necessity of being intentional.

I was doing a Bible study on Sunday nights at church, and in it I learned that I needed to be having a quiet time alone with God every morning. This would mean that I would have to be intentional about setting an alarm and getting up before my family. I decided to try it; I mean, it couldn't hurt. August 2005 was when I started having my quiet time. It was a Sunday night, and I was determined to get up the next morning before anyone else in my house. That evening was far from smooth; the kids wouldn't go to bed, and one of them ended up with a nose bleed. I wasn't going to let that stop me. That morning was the first small step towards the light.

So, here I am, almost fifteen years later. I have taken many small steps that have forever changed my path. Intentionally setting my alarm every morning has helped me to prioritize my faith and my spiritual practice so I can immerse myself in my full life.

I am now in my second year as an elementary school principal. My kids are nineteen and sixteen. And while there are still times that life is chaotic, I know with absolute certainty that being intentional in prioritizing my faith above everything else has had the greatest return on investment—not only in my life but also in the lives of my family and those I am blessed to serve at school.

+++

Leading with Faith at the Center

Faith: In this space, you make room for spiritual practices that sustain, grow, and develop your spiritual maturity.

Now it could easily be argued that faith falls squarely in the personal quadrant, and we definitely reference this in the original text, as well as when bringing this message to organizations. I have found that placing faith in the center, however, allows me to prioritize this foundation above every other, where it should be in my life, and it also doesn't crowd up that personal quadrant that is so critical for growing and setting intention.

For this section, I urge you to take time and document the big rocks in your life. I also challenge that one big rock should come from each section. That would leave five big rocks for you, but you could also identify more than five or choose not to add one from any one section. Many people identify family and health from the personal quadrant and combine professional growth into their work identity. Whatever works for you is what is best, so long as none of your biggest priorities from a blended full life viewpoint get left behind.

Rising from the Ash Pit

During the 2016–2017 school year, I began to think a lot more critically about several spaces of my life, but I was not totally immersing myself everywhere. My positional quadrant was still stealing a lot from the rest, but I was incredibly mindful about making space for my daughters. Time with them was so precious, and with the change in makeup and focus at school, I was able to devote more time to them. I had hired really well after all that turnover, and we entered into a period of steady, positive rebuilding. The interim superintendent at that time set the tone that we would be building relationships and building back trust. I was able to flourish in this space professionally because of my connections with incredible colleagues in my professional learning network, including deep connections with the team with which I worked every day. I started trying all the great leadership ideas I had been learning about, and our team worked on building up a positive climate brick by brick. I will never forget the special working connection I developed with the administrative team in that year and the one following. They became close friends and confidants, and I will forever be grateful for the trust, risk-taking, and growth we all shared together. I spent focused and intentional time getting to know staff and students with a lot less pressure. That year, I ran my first marathon, and the self-development that came out of the experience of training had a deep and propelling impact on many domains of my life. I was not quite spiritually awakened, but man was I getting there!

When my coauthors and I decided to write the book on balance, something we desperately needed for ourselves, the framework we created began to guide the ways in which I focused my energies into the quadrants. I began reading again! My husband and I had been attending church regularly, but I was starting to see the benefit of listening to more faith-filled music and considered a devotional might be something to add to my morning routine. Another marathon had me focusing on hydration and a stronger focus with nutrition. Critical focus on building back my space in the home in a more comfortable way allowed for my husband and I to repair a lot of the damage done from a lack of intentionality.

What a miracle we are living now in 2019 with all this intention! I cannot tell you what a true blessing this framework has been in my life. Intentionality allowed me to live very focused in my titled role, proved I could write a book while working full time, still keep up my running streak, offer my children more intentional time and special moments with both myself and their dad, restore a marriage to last for the long haul, and develop such a spiritual connection with my Heavenly Father that I take steps and leaps in His name. All results occurred truly from being intentional about immersing myself in my *full* life, and not just a few spaces. Wow. I had no idea what I was missing during the period of my life where striving in a leadership position meant surviving in all aspects of my life.

We are meant to have life and live it to the full. The best way to do that is to immerse ourselves in all of it!

Gift yourself with some time now to engage with the fear challenge that follows. Dive in whenever you feel is best for you, but do not allow this opportunity to intentionally identify spaces of your life where you can immerse yourself pass you by.

> *We are meant to have life and live it to the full. The best way to do that is to immerse ourselves in all of it!*

Face the Fear

Which spaces in your own life are you pouring more or less energy into with intention? Are you prioritizing your faith or letting it fit in where you can? When you consider your current level of satisfaction in regard to immersion in your full life, where are you at, and do you need to review this in more depth?

Slay the Fear

Review your current immersion in each area. Identify your big rocks so you can set intentional goals that will help you improve immersion where you need it most. Much like the five stones David gathered, the big rocks you identify here will be what you use to slay whatever stands between you and living your fullest life.

Join the conversation and share your insights on social media.
#LeadwithFAITH

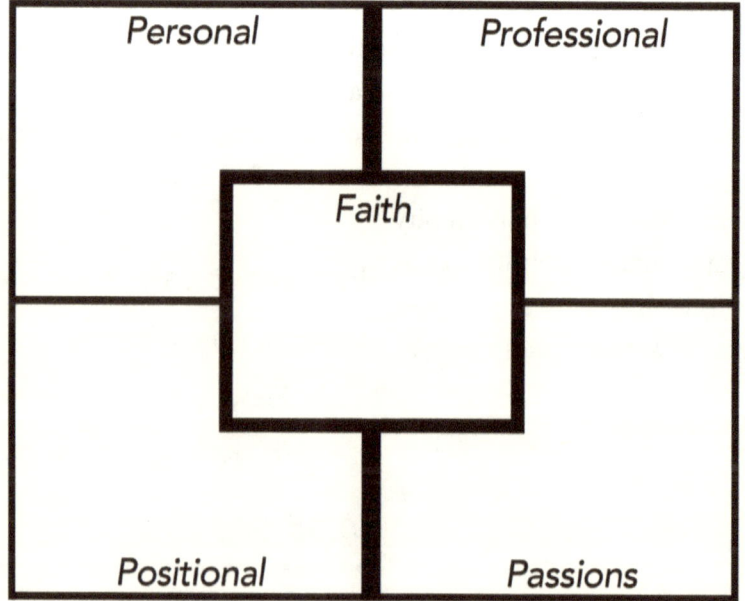

CHAPTER 8

Make Each Day Count

You can be the architect of moments that matter.
—Chip Heath, The Power of Moments

On a warm and sunny, no plans kind of July morning, as I prepared for a joyful uninterrupted day with my children, I received a text from a staff member alerting me that it was possible one of our recent graduates had passed away the prior evening. He had been hearing this from students, but he was not sure of the accuracy. The student was a quiet, unassuming, kind young man. Flashes of him coming to prom and the senior activity night looking confident and full of life popped into my mind. I recalled his brother, what his parents looked like, an interaction or two over the short year I had been leading there. An icy pit formed in my stomach as I realized the only way to confirm this possibly earth-shattering information was to call a potentially grieving parent. But how do you start a conversation like that? As a leader with three years of trials and triumphs in my repertoire at that time, I knew the answer was simple. You just start.

Though I cannot even now recall the entire conversation, how I started it, how it ended, I will most certainly never forget the content. Yes, in fact, the recent graduate was gone. His time in this life was over at eighteen years old.

Time. None of us possess enough, we lack complete and utter control over its movement and pace, and we cannot magically create more of it. A long-held life mantra of mine has come from Muhammad Ali: "Don't count the days; make the days count." There is such inspiration in this statement, wide open to individual interpretation. I truly believe in making every moment of each day count for something; however, as I sat in the pew of a funeral for that young man whose time expired far too early, I will never forget the message I heard that day from the pastor. Sharing Psalm 90:12, "Teach us to number our days that we may gain a heart of wisdom," the pastor urged us all to number our days. We must do so, lovingly, carefully, and with the knowledge that they will most certainly run out. We cannot predict the amount that will stack up by the end of our time here on earth, but we must be taught to number them.

> "Teach us to number our days that we may gain a heart of wisdom."

Up until then, I had been looking at the counting concept very differently. The year prior, I had begun to believe a sinister and ugly lie from the enemy that my home life and my husband were not exciting enough. I thought our desires for life were so vastly different, and that the lifestyle of squandering time away spent in routine fashion was sheer waste. I began behaving in ways that were not wise. Not wise at all. Foolish. And though I was not quite ready to internalize the depth of the Psalms from the pastor's lips and place the message into action until months later, I certainly heard it loud and clear: *Teach us to number our days so that we become wise in heart—not so that we live life on our terms and in wild, memorable fashion.* It's a slight difference with huge impact.

From this chapter of my life, I gift you with this revelation of my own. Believing the devil's lies may give us experience, and, if we allow, God will always turn that into wisdom.

Making days count can mean to some to blow off work and go golfing all day. After all, YOLO! Modern culture lures us into believing that our actions and beliefs around "You Only Live Once" are justifiable. Seek adventure and thrill, satiate your cravings, and live full-throttle so you can "do you." Wisdom, however, calls for a much more tempered calculation to the counting. It counsels a sage view for the long haul that takes into account the idea that we may accomplish less than the world desires of us, but that what we place in those days must be worthy, honoring, and wise hearted.

Going back to our big rocks provides an opportunity to count those days and live in wise-hearted fashion with great intention. It is not anal retentive to schedule your days. In fact, intentionally calendaring and goal setting in each of these spaces means that we make each one count by realizing our time is short, whether we get seventeen or ninety-seven years. If we are living our lives with intention meant to influence, then we've got a lot of big work to do, friends. Doing it with a wise heart means living out that legacy with intention. You can't do that by allowing your time to blow by scrolling through social media or letting opportunity to influence others pass you by. Wisdom calls for living in a way that meets the balance between restoration each day and fully fueled, pumped up, and pouring out. We cannot over- or under-commit our time on this earth, friends. Both of those practices do a disservice to the legacy we are to lead.

Let's be intentional about making those ever-precious, numbered days count.

FAITH IN ACTION
LYNMARA COLÓN, DIRECTOR, AUTHOR, VIRGINIA
@THECOLON_S

There are times in our lives that things come unexpectedly. We often think we have a lot of time to create memories, make that phone call, or let others know we love them. Maybe our hope and faith make us believe that time is eternal; getting in the way of being intentional about building relationships with those who matter most. I know this to be true, because as I navigate several griefs in my life, I can't help but reflect on how fast time has passed by and how I can make every minute left the most beautiful one.

Losing a parent brings a unique perspective to life and relationships in general. We often think about death as something that happens when we are older or very ill. Most of us do not focus on the present as we go on with our everyday lives. But losing my dad reminded me of the importance of creating memories with those we love.

As the mother of seniors in high school, I've struggled with creating moments now that they are older. For so many years I focused on planning outings to special places, buying the toys that would make them smarter, and competing to be the "Pinterest Mom." I became exhausted trying to create Facebook worthy moments that will let my family know that I had not failed at the most precious assignment I have been given. Not too long ago, I asked my daughters "How do you know I love you?" and their answer shocked me. "Mom, we know you love us when you spend time with us." Something so simple. I had spent years trying to impress my own girls and all they wanted was for me to be present.

Seeing them prepare to leave our home has brought a sense of grief many do not talk about. Every day they need me less and I question whether or not I have done a good job to prepare them for the next chapter in their lives. Even though I know they have been raised in a home where faith and a love for Christ is our compass, I know they will soon encounter experiences that will test everything we have taught them. I've cried in silence and often prayed for wisdom to come up with the best advice when someone lets them down or they simply discover that we live in a broken world.

You do not have to physically lose someone to experience the loss of the fairy tale, the perfect moments that you dreamed of at one point. Every day we go out into a world filled with people in need of grace, kindness, and love. And while I am not perfect, and neither are my girls; my goal is to spend the little time I have before they leave me equipping them to love others and show them the love only God can shine through them. I know I can't do this alone. But I do have faith that just like God pours his love and grace on me daily; he will fulfill His promise of taking care of my daughters. It's the best gift I can offer them while I create memories that will last a lifetime.

+++

Set Goals to Live with Intention

Look, I could go into a whole long section on why some goals get accomplished and others don't. There is truly so much motivational theory, habit research, and process issues with goal setting. As always, I will provide several resources with which I have engaged in the past to help you if you are not a goal crusher by design. What I can tell you is if you are intentional about the process in this space and look at it through a faith-filled lens, it sure is hard not to accomplish them, knowing you are created to accomplish much more than you could ask or imagine. For our goals in this section, we are simply going to focus on building growth for your intentional living in the quadrants and added faith section from the previous chapter. It's one thing to identify those big rocks. It is a whole other thing to intentionally grow in them! And that is what you are called to do in order to live your best and most faithful version, friends. You must be intentional about smashing your goals.

In the previous section, you identified your priority areas in each quadrant. If you ignored me, go back and do that now. Right now. Go back. I'll see you in a few. For the rest of you, let's forge forth in faith.

We are going to start with a priority area because if you dare try to accomplish it all at once, you are highly likely to fail. Give yourself permission to accomplish one or two goals, then add more in. You have so much freedom in this, so do not make the mistake of taking on too much. I also challenge you to go further when you reach your goals. We are meant to live fully and most vibrantly. If you are already rocking in one space, challenge yourself to grow further.

The process I am recommending has worked best for me. Obviously, you are all bright thinkers and seasoned goal setters, so go with what works for you.

Start out with placing your priorities and adding an ideal immersion action with each. Here are a couple of examples:

Personal
Daughters —> Make memories they will never forget.
Husband —> Develop our intimacy with more time together.

Now take those statements and add actions into each.
- Make memories my daughters will never forget by creating a Summer of Fun Bucket List.
- Develop intimacy with husband by scheduling and planning a weekly date experience.

Professional
Grow as a Leader —> Move from consuming to creating.
Amplify Women —> Create a space for stories with a podcast.

Actions
- Start a blog and commit to publishing once per month.
- Create a podcast which will launch one interview per week.

The beautiful part of this process is that once you start, you will realize the endless possibilities to create intention with your big rocks. Once you have actionable statements for each, it is time to create a timeline for them and place them firmly on your calendar. If these action items are something you do on a regular basis, this will be as simple as calendaring them consistently. If they represent a big action, placing a timeline on the calendar is still critical.

Because I don't know how to do life differently, I will share very vulnerably the visual of what I created through this process at this point for 2019. For me, this process was tied to a deeply spiritual direction, and my #OneWord for 2019 was #SLAY. For those unfamiliar with the post I wrote around that one word, the quick summary is that I had thought the year prior held all kinds of giants I had challenged and slayed. I left a position that I loved. I listened to the Holy Spirit's call to me to grow and develop my skills as a leader and an author. I started a podcast to amplify others. All of these actions were out of my comfort zone, and I figured they were my giants. I was reminded through this process, however, that all of those were tied to #RISE, which was my one word the year prior. The 2019 year was to be filled with more fear to overcome and many giants to #SLAY. I share these with you so you can see what your grid might look like and because part of sharing this message is sharing what God has done in my life through the work I am promoting for you to do in this text.

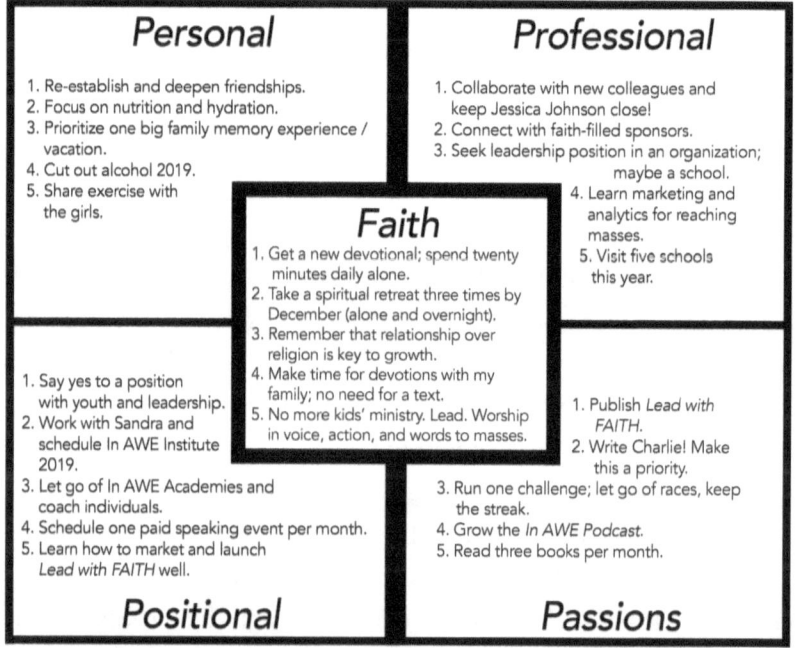

Now, to be clear, this was actually version 2.0 because I had jumped into this process a bit on autopilot. After all, the goals I had set this way the year prior came so easily, and I had simply written them in my journal. Instead of listening carefully and discerning the spiritual direction, I allowed a lot of my own human processing brain to dictate what I placed on my grid without really realizing it.

I share this with you because listening to that still small voice takes a lot of patience, practice, and trial sometimes.

I had put a decent amount of energy into placing the original items on my calendar with deadlines for many of the goals, but I will state honestly that I did not follow my schedule faithfully, and I also failed to go back to my list regularly to ensure I was hitting the big items. In April, I documented a clear direction that stated I needed to rework my #SLAY goals, and I honestly put that off until May when completing the manuscript for this text.

I share this process with you so you can see that you can also adjust expectations and strive for discernment. Continue to listen. This life of leading with faith is not a simple and one-off experience. Sometimes we make decisions that must then be altered. If we do it with a discerning mind and with our most faithful and courageous heart, we and our goals will be refined through the process.

The process of refining our focus around our big rocks is important to continuously develop, and doing so with a faith-filled focus has prompted me to accomplish more than I could ask or imagine with the confidence created in developing these focus areas in line with faith. While the example I provide is the first time I have reestablished goals in this way, I am grateful to have a humble enough spirit to do so in order that I can seek each next step in carrying them out. Ditching certain practices is so much better than clinging to something I established months prior that is not serving the best version of me. We all need to be able to prune and refine. I hope by sharing this process, you will feel permission to do the same as you develop focus areas in your own life.

After step one is complete, it is time to set some specific goals. This part is up to you in regard to how detailed you want to get. For me, I simply use these as the basis for setting up my outcomes and timelines. Again, you determine which areas you will spend time in first. There are twenty-five items on my list, but remember this is for a year's worth of life. Some are a lot easier to set goals around, and others cannot be time bound. Saying yes to a position with youth and leadership seems out of my control. This is a big rock placeholder that I will not set a goal around, but I will review these items all year to remind myself. For a goal, let's look at one that requires much more thought and focus: "Schedule one paid speaking event per month."

My action steps from that statement include active research and marketing my speaking services. It means that I will need to develop materials to share my services, and that I will need to reach out to organizations in an active way rather than wait to be contacted. Admittedly, this is not comfortable for me, but given the fact that this is an explicit action on my goals, I will do it. One statement like this: "Schedule one paid speaking event per month by the end of July 2019."

Action Steps

1. Create marketing flier and update website for potential schedulers to review.
2. Research events that need a keynote in months at least six months out. Contact conference schedulers with flier and speaker one page.
3. Contact personnel in charge of professional development in organizations with flier and speaker one page.
4. Develop video promotional materials from footage to share on my site as well as with potential schedulers.
5. By August 2019, have each month in the year covered with a paid speaking contract in hand.
6. Reach out to trusted mentors and sponsors for assistance and recommendations if unable to secure any given month and ask for referrals or advice.

With each of my big rock focused statements, I go through each to prioritize like this. Some can be "accomplished," and others are ongoing, requiring daily intentional focus. For both, I recommend setting your calendar with intention.

Schedule Priorities with Intentionality

Leading in life and at work requires us to be intentional about our time so we let none of it slip by without our permission. We all have the same number of hours in each day and days in the week. In order to live them out with intention, we must calendar with intention. This is something I did not put fully into practice until I made the commitment to take hold of my days. As Covey says, "The key is not to prioritize what is on your schedule, but to schedule your priorities." Do not let that wisdom pass you by. Savor its richness in simplicity and truth.

In leadership, you will find there are blocks of each day you cannot get around. Depending upon your role in any organization, you may have more or less flexibility to schedule your priorities. The key is to take the space that does belong to you and maximize it with your priorities. If for you that means 5:00 a.m. until 6:30 a.m. and not again until 5:00 p.m. until 10:00 p.m., you still have 6.5 hours of each day for autonomous intentionality. I also push you to consider which spaces in the day belong to you for scheduling priorities. If you are a teacher and your priority is to grow professionally and need to fit reading in, calendar reading time once per week during lunch or prior to the bell. If you are a school leader, and your priority is building relationships, then build a system of intentionality during lunch supervision. And if you are one who simply stands there lording over the lunchroom, rethink this practice immediately. (See the section on Leading with Heart.) You can take hold of this lunch supervision and build relationships intentionally with each of the students in your building. Make plans to connect with each kid and staff member throughout the month. That is totally possible, and you know it. If you were calendaring interactions, it would mean you would be intentional about taking lists of students and placing them on your calendar at lunch supervision. Even better? Delegate this task to your administrative assistant and have that individual schedule a relationship connection for each day of the year, whether that is at lunch, arrival, dismissal, or passing times. You can be intentional and make a large impact while not taking on the sand task of scheduling.

Batching your work is of high recommendation as a practice for your calendaring priorities. The simple definition of batching is that you dedicate a block of time where you will work in a focused and intentional manner to complete the related items without distraction (email, text, social media, phone calls, etc.) Batching tasks allows you to train your brain to focus on completion and be more efficient with your time. There is some very compelling research out there that tells us we need to provide ourselves focused space to create, think deeply, and complete our work. According to one study, our productivity decreases by 40 percent if we allow ourselves to "multitask," and the truth is that we aren't multitasking. We are simply switching quickly from one process to another and being efficient at none of it. In her book, *Bored and Brilliant*, Manoush Zomorodi shares that we take an average of twenty-three minutes and fifteen seconds to get back into deep thinking work when we allow distraction, both self-imposed and driven by others. In my case, distractions feel constant because we have a new puppy in addition to email, texts, desire to get on Twitter, Instagram, or Facebook to be relevant. If we are to be efficient, deep thinking, and leaders that get work completed, we must be intentional about minimizing distraction. Countless resources exist to assist you with this process if you need more external motivation, but the solution can truly present as simple as planning out your workflow, setting a timer, and committing to the work for that amount of time without distraction. It will be amazing what you can accomplish when you work in this way! Also, be sure to build in circuit breakers. If you are like me, you will want to just keep working through the time, especially if you complete your batch in the designated amount of time. Just remember that your brain needs a break, and plowing through won't necessarily increase productivity either. Set intentions and finish, friends.

Here is an example of what my schedule looks like these days, but please keep in mind, as an entrepreneur, my days are very flexible. Honestly, because of that freedom, I have found that I must be more intentional with my time. The autonomy can be freeing, but a lack of focus leads to chasing any old squirrel that passes and a frightening amount of delay. On the other end, I can also fall into the trap of oversaturating my brain and not taking any breaks if I

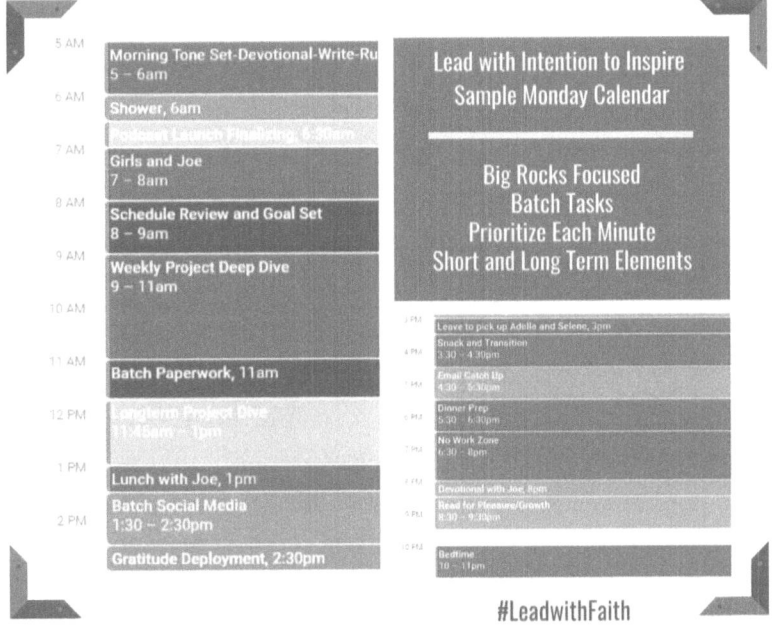

#LeadwithFaith

do not create a plan. Important note is that this is a typical representation, but there are also several ways I need to adjust depending upon a wide range of reasons. I've shown it here simply to illustrate prioritizing your schedule and batching.

If scheduling your life this way feels overwhelming at first, start small. Select certain times to place priority first until you are used to following these actions. More likely than not, you will find that living with intention is the ultimate way to free up a lot more of your time both at home and work, allowing you to add more passion projects or down time with loved ones or alone in your schedule.

Number your days to increase your wisdom as a person who leads with faith. Placing intention in your day will allow you to be more to others, yourself, and propel you to intentionally build your legacy while you are living it.

Face the Fear

When it comes to goal setting, what has tripped you up in the past in regard to finishing? Are you a person who starts well and does not finish? Do you struggle adjusting something once you have committed? In regard to scheduling, do you feel unable to prioritize? Name any blockage that you have now so you can determine ways to get around them.

Slay the Fear

One by one, consider each of the big rocks you identified in the previous chapter and develop a goal for prioritizing it. Begin this process with one that you see as your most important priority. Create a plan and schedule time on your calendar to accomplish this high-priority goal.

Join the conversation and share your insights on social media.
#LeadwithFAITH

CHAPTER 9

Practice Gratitude to Inspire and Build Up Others

*Gratitude for the seemingly insignificant—a seed—
this plants the giant miracle.*

—Ann Voskamp

At the start of the 2016–2017 school year, influenced by an incredible group of women leaders, MAPS (Moms as Principals), I went out on a limb to lead my building into a state of practiced gratitude, in the hopes that it would build up our climate, and to introduce more of my own personality and style of leadership that had been watered down in the two years prior by circumstance, fear, and culture. It was a risk, but it was one I took to with zest and deep hope that I could impact my staff in ways that would create a ripple effect in the building. I never measured the results, and I did not have a plan for calculating the effect. It was not scientific, but it had a grounding in research, a focus on intention, and the results could have been correlational, but I know they were noticeable.

As a person and a leader, I was entering into a season of autonomy, growth, and a high need to live authentically in all spaces. Despite the fact that we had just come off a rough couple of years, I knew we were ready to begin building back a sense of community, and with my entire building staffed and ready to rock, I decided to go big on intention and gratitude. While the MAPS group was made up of primarily elementary principals, I was working with a team made up of secondary professionals, so I decided to change up the suggestions and add some depth, keeping the spirit of the "Worth It Box" intact. Prior to the start of the school year, I purchased photo boxes from our local Hobby Lobby in a mix of distinct patterns and solid colors to meet the preferences of our team members as much as possible. My incredibly talented lead admin assistant worked alongside me to fill the boxes with school branded items. I then handwrote each of my staff members a sincere and authentic message of gratitude to start the year. These were ready to be handed out as we began the last part of our time together before we welcomed students back. I will never forget the charge of the room that day. After we had spent time learning and planning, goal setting, and focusing on our curriculum and instruction and welcome back activities, I launched in.

I started out sharing with the staff Chase Mielke's incredible YouTube video, "Is Teaching Worth It?", where he poetically weaves the challenges of teaching, as well as the triumphs, to powerfully remind us of our purpose with students. After the power in that message, the staff had the chance to share with colleagues what they were looking forward to this year with students and what made teaching worth it to them. Our shared experience was wonderful because we had a lot of new staff members that year, and it gave them all an opportunity to get to know one another's purpose in teaching in a low-profile way. I then shared with them the research I had been learning related to positive psychology and our personal well-being. I related with passion the concept that happiness can be grown with intention, and I shared with them Shawn Achor's TED Talk on "The Happiness Advantage." We discussed his points on gratitude being one of the most impactful ways we can increase our own happiness, as well as the well-being of those in our sphere of influence. Specifically, we got jazzed up about building in opportunity for them to focus on their own gratitude practices and build practices into their classroom for students. It was so joyful to witness their interactions and their own ideas floating to the top with how they could be intentional about building in happiness in their own lives.

Then I shared the boxes. They were each to grab a box based upon their own flair, and I was elated the teacher whom I had purchased the box of mustaches for selected that very one! I asked for a volunteer to read a poem about the value of our work aloud, and I got choked up when the individual who was reading voice cracked with emotion.

Maybe my memory of the moment has been embellished by time, but I know I saw other faces in the room with tears welled in their eyes. I took that moment to share my role that year would be to intentionally provide them little boosts of happiness to give them that advantage. I would intentionally show them gratitude for the work they did with kids, which was so worth it, and that I would be helping them be intentional in gratitude throughout the year as well.

Maybe it was before they started to leave, or maybe it was after I had handed out each individual note from my heart, but I recall one of the veteran staff members verbalizing that this was the best start to the year he'd ever had. I knew in that moment that the research was all right. Intentional gratitude invites joy into our lives and the lives of others.

Intentional gratitude invites joy into our lives and the lives of others.

FAITH IN ACTION
ROMAN NOWAK, EDUCATOR
AND FOUNDER OF BUILDHOPEEDU

*"Start each day with a positive thought
and a grateful heart."*

—Roy Bennett

When we think about making a difference in the lives of others or influencing any organization or culture, I always consider how important it is for people to build each other up. Oftentimes, in the constant rush of everyday life, one forgets how important it is to practice gratitude. Taking the time to honor someone who has done something for us or for others has unimaginable benefits.

It is important, however, to be intentional. Gratitude cannot be practiced as a single event; it needs to be ever-present in everything we do. Values such as gratitude, kindness, hope, and empathy need to be foundational elements that help guide our everyday actions. In schools, they must also be the foundational steps of mission statements, school improvement plans, and classroom rules.

As a teacher, I try to model this anytime I am with my students or my colleagues. To me, gratitude does not have to be a grand gesture, nor does it have to always be linked with a tangible or expensive object. Sharing gratitude with others involves sharing your heart: taking the time to stop and talk to others, asking them about their evening or their day, asking about their dinner plans, wishing people a good day, intentionally stopping by to see others who are not on your usual path, asking about family, having lunch with someone, bringing a coffee, or leaving a note sharing with someone how important they are or what unique talents they have. These are all various ways of practicing gratitude.

When you share gratitude, you are not necessarily thanking them for an action they did toward you; rather, you are expressing gratitude for the amazing person they are, for what they bring to your life and organization. Kids, students, and other adults look to what we do as an example. I strongly believe that if we say gratitude is important, we must be intentional about showing it on a daily basis.

> *"In everything give thanks; for this is the will of God in Christ Jesus for you."*
> —1 Thessalonians 5:18, NKJV

I am extremely grateful for the amazing people in my life who help remind me of the importance of kindness, of spreading HOPE, and leading with my heart. To my family, my wife and daughters, to my incredible PLN and Twitter family who have helped me grow as a leader and person, thank you! It is people who help us become better, and it is in people that we need to believe and invest.

> *"Gratitude can transform common days into thanksgivings, turn routine jobs into joy, and change ordinary opportunities into blessings."*
> —William Arthur Ward

+++

Go Beyond an Attitude of Gratitude

Honestly, if you don't already possess a heart for gratitude, you will need to cultivate one before you are able to lead others to deploy gratitude. Convincing you of being intentional with gratitude is one of my greatest hopes from this section. It is not flaky or new age. There is faith-filled grounding in this practice of gratitude. As one of my ultimate she-roes Brené Brown states so eloquently, "Practicing gratitude invites joy into our lives." Gratitude is a spiritual practice; you cannot have joy without gratitude. I also want to make sure you understand that my 2016 version was a bit off. I cultivated happiness, while the aim was to boost happiness, and I have since learned and believe to the root of my hairs what Brené Brown says about happiness versus joy. Happiness is circumstantial, where joy is a state of being. Happiness is to climate what joy is to culture. And if we want to build a lasting effect here, we need to be intentional with our gratitude, friends. I had a great start! And over the two years after that launch, I am happy to report that I was intentional about building this habit for my staff (though I wish I had done even more). As I related in the first chapter, my default is joyful, and it is not hard for me to display an attitude of gratitude, but that only gets us so far. It is circumstantial and can be changed based on the fluctuation of circumstance. If we are to lead with intention and influence others to live this way, we better grasp something more profound and lasting, more able to withstand the storms of climate change in a building or our lives. We must deploy gratitude and practice it daily in order to build our joy and the capacity of others. This take practice. It takes intention.

> *We must deploy gratitude and practice it daily in order to build our joy and the capacity of others.*

Here are a few ideas I have implemented, as well as some I have seen along the way. Friends, there are no shortages here, only the limitations you allow for practicing gratitude in your life. Because I know you will all be at different spaces in your lives on this, I am dividing the section into tips for self and tips for influence. Here's the deal: Once you have mastered practicing gratitude in your own life, you can easily move any one of those into the column of influence by encouraging those with whom you live and lead to do the same! Helping develop others is a foundation for leadership, and leading with faith pushes you to move beyond the fear of what others may think of you for taking professional development time for this purpose (for example, loading up a bunch of photo album boxes with a poem and a handwritten note). Risks come with rewards that are sometimes unseen. You will not lose with these.

In addition to providing the Worth It Box, I added to it all year with an intentional note at varied times throughout the year to each staff member, and I also provided branded notes for staff to use as well. If that is a challenge, there is no need to get too fancy, and my admin assistant was the one who designed and printed them all in-house. With so many options these days, you really can't go wrong, and I use Canva to create and print with Vistaprint (They often have deals!).

Throughout the year, I would be sure to provide blank note cards to encourage staff to give them to one another and to students, and I made sure to regularly do the same. I'll never forget the perfect example of modeling when I went around to hand deliver notes one day to staff, and a student said, "Do I get one of those?" When I explained it is a simple note, she indicated she wanted one, even from the principal. And you bet she got one! We cannot underestimate the importance of gratitude.

Taking this a step further, we can also see that appreciation is best received in ways the receiver understands. Much like *The Five Love Languages* in our personal relationships, we must consider the variety of ways people in our workspaces best receive gratitude. Some will want words of affirmation, others appreciate gifts, some simply want time with you, others appreciate being served, and sometimes our people need a high-five or a physical pat on the back. I am supposed to tell you not to hug in the workplace, but a well-placed, appropriate hug should never lose its effect in our world. I refuse to become jaded on this one. Just be smart, people.

To differentiate appreciation, my attempt was to have all staff complete a survey that indicated their favorites: treat, snack, beverage, place to receive a five-dollar gift card, T-shirt size, home address, etc. This way, I could methodically gift my staff throughout the year with their favorites, and it was a true treasure seeing them light up when they received their favorite, most often forgetting they had told me about it. One option I have never tried but would use to modify this attempt again would be using the "Motivation By Appreciation Inventory from Appreciation At Work." This survey is derived from the book *Five Languages of Appreciation in the Workplace.* An assessment like this could help to get a solid handle on the ways each staff member best communicates and receives appreciation. What a solid investment and a perfect way to be intentional in showing our appreciation to each of our team members.

If you need a kickstart for ideas, here are a few more ideas to get you deploying that gratitude!

Practicing Gratitude to Develop Self

1. Gratitude statements you say out loud or in your mind repeatedly.
2. Gratitude journal: Start with three statements per day, then try to get to 1,000 like author Ann Voskamp!
3. Gratitude time each day: Calendar a time to mindfully focus on your gratitude.
4. Text messages of gratitude to loved ones, colleagues, friends, and others each day.
5. Handwritten notes with authentic appreciation at home or at work.
6. Daily emails of gratitude to at least one person.
7. Social media posts with tags to people to show gratitude.
8. Select staples for which you are grateful and create a visual, then display it somewhere in your home or workspace and set time to state these out loud every day: "I am grateful for _____."
9. Designate a specific list of people to whom you want to express gratitude, and deploy it in whatever way you want, but be sure to check them off the list.
10. Keep a list of moments in the work day and write them as you feel grateful instead of waiting until journal time.

Practicing Gratitude to Influence Others

1. Provide note cards (branded or blank) to staff and set aside time at a staff meeting to write out a note of gratitude to a colleague, student, or other person. Gift them with the means and the time to do it!

2. Develop a building climate goal to increase joy through gratitude; use a survey you create or invest in the Motivation By Appreciation Inventory linked in the resource section and be sure staff understand their colleagues' preferred language. Create a building goal where individuals develop their own gratitude deployment goals and review progress with one another.

3. Create an opportunity for students to show gratitude! Through a classroom project, club, character-building initiative, or other means relative to your organization, bring students in on the action!

4. Encourage and create space for those in your life to deploy gratitude at home. Model this yourself, instituting some type of system that encourages family members to practice gratitude (see above for ideas to start) or create a daily family opportunity to share what they were grateful for in the day. Keep it simple to start and watch it flourish as the consistency develops!

5. Go the extra mile! Contact a family member for each of your staff members. Use whichever method is most comfortable to you, but share your gratitude for their service in your organization. It could be their spouse, children, parents, or siblings. Collecting this information can be as simple as asking in a Google Form or delegating some investigative work to your administrative assistant. I promise you—the impact will last and be so special for all of you. Example: "Thank you for sharing

Suzie with us! I know her hard work at school is important to her, and her talents are so appreciated here. She is a blessing to me each day as our school counselor, and she brings great joy to our work environment. We are so lucky that you share your mom with us every day at school."

6. Create a system for thanking parents for their awesome kids! A great way to do this is to start a "good news call of the day." I wish I had made the space for this practice a lot sooner! Bring your staff in on a reverse office referral. Have them submit when they see students doing something helpful, where it was, the day, and a brief description. Call the student in and share the news, call home with the student on speaker, being sure to express gratitude for the students' great choices, and share which teacher noticed. Send the teacher a brief description of the joy in the call. (Bring the teacher in if you are able, but remember not to add undue burden on any of you in carrying this out, or it won't happen, and your system misses out on the effects of constantly carrying out this gratitude.) Check out the hashtag #Goodnewscalloftheday for inspiration!

7. At home: Create a gratitude board in your home that all family members can contribute to and see. Be sure to stock it when others' stores seem empty, but also be sure to encourage everyone to participate. Consistency and visibility will have a lasting impact—guaranteed! Note: You could do this in the staff workroom or even hallway displays for students to add to as they are led.

8. Influence up and out by providing opportunities for the board of education, district personnel, parents, and community to show gratitude. Make it simple by sending out a newsletter that offers a consistent opportunity to express specific gratitude to the school or members of the staff. Share these with the

individuals, either at staff meetings or privately, if they prefer. Go further by having shout outs on your social media pages from these submissions.

9. Create space in your staff meetings to share gratitude to start. Model it first, then watch it grow. Encourage staff to share the simple things for which they are grateful to the large things. No need to one up. Sometimes, we are grateful that a particular student shows up at school for three days in a row!

10. If you engage with the Worth It Box or a variation, create space throughout the year or, at a minimum, close up the school year by having the staff bring the box or a selected message from the box and develop a chance to share it. Make this meaningful from start to finish! Depending upon the culture of your staff, you could have small group shares or have the expectation that everyone shares. Be sure to note the amount of gratitude and the impact regifting these messages to one another has on the group.

There are at least twenty ideas curated right here for you! Living with intention in this space holds the potential to shift mindsets and create a lasting ripple. It is research and evidenced based. Leading with faith in this case creates intentional legacy building by taking risks to be different and disrupting our default patterns in life. What a great risk to take!

Face the Fear

Do you struggle with showing appreciation to others, or have you tried before and not received affirmation? When you consider your own context, how could you take any of these ideas and make them work in your own environment in a way that is courageous yet comes from your own heart?

Slay the Fear

Create an intentional system to show gratitude at home or at work. Bonus for you if you do it in both spaces!

Join the conversation and share your insights on social media.
#LeadwithFAITH

GATHERING STONES

- **Appreciation at Work-Motivation by Appreciation Inventory**: https://www.appreciationatwork.com/work-personality-test/
- *7 Habits of Highly Effective People* by Stephen Covey
- *Balance Like a Pirate: Going Beyond Work-Life Balance to Ignite Passion and Thrive as an Educator* by Jessica Cabeen, Jessica Johnson, and Sarah Johnson
- *Bored and Brilliant* on New York Public Radio: wnyc.org/series/bored-and-brilliant
- **Chase Mielke's "Is Teaching Worth It" video**: youtube.com/watch?v=bySSgjbjqqw
- **Shawn Achor's TEDxTalk: "The Happiness Advantage"**: youtube.com/watch?v=GXy__kBVq1M
- **Miss Decarbo's "It's Worth It Box"**: missdecarbo.com/its-worth-it-box-free-poem-printable

SECTION FOUR

Transcend Titles and Embrace Transformation

*Leadership is not about titles, positions, or flowcharts.
It is about one life influencing another.*

—John Maxwell

Transcending Titles and Embracing Transformation Foundations

- If service is beneath you, then leadership is beyond you.
- If we worship the idol of a title, we lead with fear that losing it means we lose our identity.
- Leaders are more than their titles. We can lead from anywhere.
- Leading with faith means we embrace transformation in ourselves and work to impact the transformation of our systems.
- True leadership transcends titles and allows us to transform others and ourselves through humble service.

My father never held a high-level, fancy title in an organization, but he has long been the role model I look to for true leadership. He was not the "firstborn" in his family, and there is no title for the second son in a family. He worked hard on the farm, even going so far as to redo his siblings' chores because, as he tells it, he saw doing work in excellence as a form of showing love to the animals. He did not complete high school but began working on his dad's farm after tenth grade. He served there daily, getting paid less than his cohorts who worked on other farms. After meeting my mom, he began to dream differently for his life and he made a decision to work for someone other than his family. That's when he experienced a taste of what his leadership could do. It was not long before he was elevated in title as a youth, simply due to his devoted work ethic and thoroughness. He was crafty with his hands, and one illustration of his value was when he saved the farm owner thousands of dollars in repairs on an expensive field machine he had broken in a rookie mistake. He owned the mistake, and he worked tirelessly to fix it, which earned him the title of foreman.

In 1964, Dad answered his call to leadership in one of the most inspirational ways when he enlisted in the U.S. Army. He was in love with a young woman five years his junior, and he knew he needed to lead in his personal life too. So his answer was that he would serve—willingly. Not wanting to wait for a draft, he wanted to do it on his own terms. He was not a lifer, but he was a leader in this way. He was told his desire was too small for the Air Force, and since he wanted to be done in two years, the Army it was. With disdain, the recruiter told him all he would be was a grunt where he could be an officer in the Air Force. With a keen and focused eye, my dad signed on the line to serve as a "grunt." He committed to two years of service without even confirming with his parents or fiancée.

When I picture the conversation between my parents, I get emotional thinking about the courage it would take to leave the farm, to leave his home, to leave the love of his life, to leave his parents, knowing that his younger siblings looked to him as a steady leader in the home. His heart had always been way too big for this sacrifice not to mean something to him deeply.

While serving in Vietnam, my dad missed his own graduation because he was serving by driving around the commander and the families of those who attended the ceremony. Such humility.

He credits a commanding officer who helped him through some challenging times when he and my mom struggled with the expected challenges of those circumstances. My dad focused the best he could on bettering himself in every way, finishing his high school equivalency while serving.

My dad has always gone the extra mile for people, and his humility makes him magnetic and trusted. I have to assume that it was because of his attention to detail and willingness to do what others have to be asked, my dad's service may have been made safer for him. Instead of being right on the line while in Vietnam, he drove officers around. Yes, this was dangerous, but as he tells it, this was also a relative win because it allowed him to travel and work on the vehicles, something he loved.

Life led my father to a variety of places, and he has led each day of his life with humility and resisting the idol of a title. Though he was a successful business owner for decades, he never called himself a CEO or founder. He simply owned and operated the business, building upon lead after lead and loyal customer after loyal customer for over thirty years. In a twilight career, he worked humbly delivering beds for Select Comfort and mentored men of all ages, resisting the request to become a manager, but still mentoring his coworkers. He resisted the idol of a title and simply led through service and humility.

In our home, his leadership came with a title of Dad, but to be honest, he resisted that idol pretty well, deferring it to God, the Heavenly Father, as the most important. The weight of his authority was ever-present, but his consistent, humble, loving heart is what still wins respect from us and from the dozens of "adopted" kids, grandkids, and extended family branches that long for the shade in his steady and comforting leadership.

He didn't hold a weighty title at church, but you can bet he had countless mentees and others of all types—younger and older, male and female, believers and nonbelievers—that he impacted throughout his life. No need for a title. His model is where I have taken a page from his book recently.

In the gap from my principal title to where I am now, I have served at church in youth ministry as an assistant to the teacher, a lead teacher, a donut deliverer, and now as a worship team member. I am not in charge in any of these spaces, rather I lead by allowing others to shine, serving at my best in whatever role I'm scheduled for, and staying faithful in the little things that matter so we can all function well. This service space is growing me larger in leadership than I could have asked, simply by reminding me that we don't need titles to serve well.

> *True leadership transcends titles and allows us to transform others and ourselves through humble service.*

As my earthly father has taught me over and over and over, it's not the title that makes you a leader but your actions. It's not your official responsibility that gives you the authority to impact those around you. It's not your circumstances and a particular designation that calls you to be a light or of service to anyone in your sphere. True leadership transcends titles and allows us to transform others and ourselves through humble service.

DAVID TRANSCENDED TITLES AND TRANSFORMED

Though David was not perfect, he did lead beyond his title, often fighting directly in battle, and deferring to God consistently with his plans. A perfect example that we can look to for humility in David is in his example of collecting for thirteen years all the items that Solomon would need to build the temple for God. David could have used his title of king to override this command, yet he yielded his station and earthly desire to God and served in this way.

When your days are over and you go to be with your ancestors, I will raise up your offspring to succeed you, one of your own sons, and I will establish his kingdom. He is the one who will build a house for me, and I will establish his throne forever.

—1 Chronicles 17:11–12, NIV

CHAPTER 10

Servant Leadership or Martyrdom?

Everybody can be great because everybody can serve. You don't have to have a college degree to serve. You don't have to make your subject and your verb agree to serve. You only need a heart full of grace, a soul generated by love.

—Martin Luther King, Jr.

We would be hard pressed to find a more service-oriented leader than Jesus Christ. In his example, we see a leader who had every reason to act in a haughty manner around his titles, "Son of God," "Savior of the World," "King of Kings." I mean, consider the reality of his story for a minute. If anyone had reason to saunter around, proud of a title on this Earth, we could all agree that his was of highest order, yet serve he did. Instead of relying upon legions of servants and leaning on his title to save himself from betrayal and a painful, torturous, humiliating death, he led with love and service to the end. He washed the feet of the sinful and cast off, he regularly elevated the station of the oppressed around him, and he got his hands into what others considered dirty, serving and leading each day through his stories and acts of service. I don't care who you are in an organization; you will never be labeled the Prince of Peace or Light of the World.

Yet we get so caught up in our titles.

When I first got my own classroom, I distinctly remember telling my superintendent how excited I was to share the nameplate on the door and the website with my parents. They would see my name tied to this title! (Joke was on me when I learned I wouldn't have my own classroom for the first two years, teaching from a cart and sharing other rooms.) The very title of "Teacher" was so hard-fought and earned that the shininess and status of it admittedly allured me—for a while. As I was taught to place titles on my resumés, and as the world gave way to technology platforms where titles were the first thing people saw of me, the idol of a title became increasingly challenging to resist. Yes, I will admit becoming a wife mattered to me, as did layering on the title of mom. These were all precious, infinitely sacred, and the latter came with many painful years of working hard for what seemed to come so easy to others. Yet, like any title we layer on, the weight of it can start to bind us, and we begin to become quite territorial over those titles, shifting in and out of importance depending upon the context.

When I received the official title of principal after holding the dream in my heart since long before I even graduated with my bachelor's degree, there was a slice of pride that was all mine. After all, I had a signature stamp! Though my name is nothing exciting, there are thousands of Sarah Johnsons, this title distinguished me in a way others didn't. The title illustrated the dedication to developing myself into a titled leader who had worked countless hours to complete coursework, experience hours, and several interviews before I was finally given a contract four years after completing my degree! A young, blonde woman in her twenties is a candidate people in my neck of the woods "take a risk on" in hiring. The responsibility of the persistently earned title was one I relished and took quite seriously—so much, in fact, that the heavy responsibility

I tied to the title started making me believe that it was my most important label.

Don't get me wrong. I think I remained humble enough about it, especially by outward measures. When my mom would introduce me to people as a principal, I would get a bit embarrassed with their shift in reverie and wonder. I tried hard not to lead with that information in any new connection because being a principal comes with a lot of baggage that people have associated with the title, mostly "The Disciplinarian." So it's not really that I idolized the title for its societal value; though I have definitely uncovered the shelter it provides once I ripped it off my name, feeling lost without it for quite a while.

The idolization came in the service, my friends, and a fallible belief in what was required of me to be a servant leader. I am not a perfect servant leader, walking around in human form, blessed in perfection. I am weak, human, prone to exhaustion and depletion. I do not have endless stores of emotional and physical capacity to give at that level without intentionally restoring myself. My relationships cannot withstand idolizing that title to the degree that I did for a period, with all the board meetings, athletic events, community gatherings, evening discipline hearings, hours of after-school meetings, morning meetings, staff climate building, and the constant focus on balancing new initiatives with what was already running, planting seeds of transformation, and building culture. Add to all that the ceaseless thinking about the people—the students, the parents, and the staff. All of these great acts left me less of a mom but striving hardest to retain this title most, less of a wife and losing ground without even realizing it, less of a daughter, especially in the spiritual sense, less of a person with an identity outside of my title.

Truthfully, I loved to serve. I started to believe the lie that I was the only one able to carry the responsibility in the details. After all, there is so much to the title that you only really understand if you've carried the weight of it. I believe that to the depths of my spirit. And I didn't know how not to do my best, which often didn't even feel good enough on my best days.

Just like we lose our name to a Mrs. or Mr. in the classroom, I began to lose it to Principal Johnson. Plain and straight. I started to forget that I was anything else other than that title and mom. I let relationship ties loosen, including those with my spouse, my siblings, my friends. I lost touch with prior coworkers and local friends, retaining only one because of the role.

Friends, I loved this role and still love this role. There is nothing like the nuances of being a building principal, and my love for it has nothing to do with ego. It has everything to do with the privilege it is to serve in this complex capacity.

One of the most critical lessons I have gained in the gap of my time away from the formal title, however, is that we can still serve regardless of our title.

Of course I knew this before I was a titled leader. After all, my whole life has been composed of leadership experiences, some carried out with an official title and others in a moment where titles meant nothing, just as I saw my dad do countless times. I have long understood that leadership can simply be starting new traditions, speaking my heart and mind out loud, modeling a new skill, sharing strategies with a coworker, or holding the door when there is absolutely no need to, other than being a loving human.

I had forgotten those nuances in the silent idolization. Maybe it started when I was "promoted" from elementary principal to middle/high so the district I was in could keep me from interviewing in my home district. Maybe idolization increased every time I made the choice to go to work instead of staying home when I was sick and accomplished important work through ailments, or when I checked emails at any time of the day and night, losing sleep over challenging circumstances at work. Possibly it was when I chose not to take days off in the summer because hiring, planning, meetings, preparation, appearances at community events, and answering to the beckoning of a boss seemed more important than planning extended vacations away for replenishment and reflection.

The simple truth is that I know our grip on titles is a universal struggle for leaders, and part of that is the context in which they serve. Add to that the fact that the phone can ring any time with an emergency, regardless of whether it is 11:00 p.m. or the middle of church on Sunday, and the responsibility in the title is ever-present, requiring you to drop it all and head in.

It's easy to idolize the title and to lose ourselves in service.

In this space of my untethering from an organization, I have learned to transcend titles in the most beautiful and blessed ways. It didn't happen right away or without a high level of refinement on my part through reflection, humility, and deconstructing the vision that my human heart had created so long ago. Without the title, I was wretched for a few months searching. I felt a bit useless, a bit less worthy, a bit less interesting, a bit less valued to the world.

And as it turns out, the stripping away of this title is one of the greatest gifts of my leap of faith.

Over time, I have been able to see how critical it is to dissociate with the idea that we are any one title. I have known that. I taught it in women's literature courses as a teacher, but I wasn't living this idea of transcending titles in my own heart. Sure, I believe in distributive leadership and made intentional efforts to share authority, though I could never fully release responsibility, but it was easy when I was the one distributing.

> *The stripping away of this title is one of the greatest gifts of my leap of faith.*

Since I left the formal, full-time title of principal, I have played around with several: author, speaker, educational consultant, adjunct professor, podcaster, entrepreneur. (That last one takes me three times every time to spell accurately.) What a perfect illustration of how our titles are only a piece of who we are anyway, none meant to be fully expressive of our whole spirits.

We are human. We aren't perfect. Why in the world would we try to be servant leaders that blur the line into self-destructive martyrdom? Even Jesus took time for silence and alone time and meaningful collaboration with his cohorts aside from the masses he served. Even Jesus went to his Father with a request to be saved prior to the sacrifice.

We are not to be martyred in our servant leadership. Resist that idol of a title. Some are too hard to spell anyway.

FAITH IN ACTION
MEGAN ANDERSON, FOURTH GRADE ELA/SS TEACHER AND EDUCATIONAL EFFECTIVENESS COACH, DYNAMIX LLC, OHIO
@MRZANDERSONWCH

"Uh . . ." Brielle, our child of God daughter, who was born with a rare genetic mutation, pointed in a determined manner to the crystal-clear shower doors as we tiredly stood together side-by-side in the bathroom.

I remember this scene from a few months ago all too crystal clear. I was a mother who was physically and emotionally worn out from working two different educational positions, and being a wife and mommy. Numerous hospital stays between our daughter's seizures and constant battles with pneumonia constantly kept creeping in like a Florida storm, sunny one second then turning into a hard, quick and ferocious rain in the blink of an eye.

I could barely open my eyelids, let alone the shower door to get ready for work that day.

"Uh," Brielle's petite little pointer finger motioned again to the shower. For a child who doesn't talk, I knew her language well.

"Do you want to take a shower with me?" I asked, even though I knew what her answer was going to be.

"Yeah!" she shouted, as her infectious, sweet grin pierced my heart with joy. She was so excited and, if those crystal-clear shower doors were a crystal ball, God had provided her with a vision happening before her very own eyes that I didn't see coming.

To be honest, I was selfishly really hoping if I took my time, she might forget. I thought this ten-to-fifteen-minute hot, relaxing shower was my "me" time to refresh, all by myself.

Finally, I slipped one foot and then the other into the shower and then grabbed Brielle's hand with a steady grip. And as I stood there, I began to weep. I wasn't upset about our current situation; I was just weary, worn out, exhausted, dog tired, but the way the shower head was directed at me allowed the droplets to sprinkle my face in the right direction. It hid my tears, it hid my tired eyes, and it hid every emotion I was feeling as I prayed for strength and whispered to myself, "You can do this, you can do this." I simply needed my faith and knew that only God could carry me through. Out of the corner of my weeping eyes, I saw Brielle slowly steady herself so she wouldn't fall, lean over, and carefully grab the bar of soap.

In my mind I thought this was such a proud mommy moment to see her take the soap and wash herself like an independent child, but then as she placed the pink marbleized soap in her tiny hands, I felt the true presence of God at that very moment. She didn't begin washing herself, but with a servant's mentality and heart, she began to wash my feet. Yes, she was washing my feet.

She took her time, from the very tips of my toes up to my ankle and then to the next foot. She took her time and, as I looked down at the beautiful scene God had placed before me, I heard Him say, "I know you are tired, and you have been serving my child for five years; it's time to let her serve you."

My exhausted tears changed into tears of renewal and strength and, as much as I thought I needed those few minutes to myself, what I really needed was to feel and be reminded how our service will leave a lasting legacy in the lives of others, just like Brielle had done for me that day. Today, leaders, I want to encourage you to simply take the time to "wash someone's feet." Find the good in every situation to encourage, inspire, and love them with an agape love like Jesus.

"Now that I, your Lord and Teacher, have washed your feet, you also should wash one another's feet. I have set you an example that you should do as I have done for you."

—John 13:14–15, NIV

+++

Face the Fear

Is there anything in this section that nestled in your gut, either from relatability or judgment? When someone asks what you do, how do you immediately respond, and why is that? After reading this section, is there anything you would change about that? Why or why not?

Slay the Fear

Visualize yourself without your paid position or the role you most readily list when someone asks what you do. How can you answer in the face of that scenario? Commit to creating a response, and practice using it.

Join the conversation and share your insights on social media.
#LeadwithFAITH

CHAPTER 11
Leadership That Transforms

Let perseverance finish its work so that you may be mature and complete, not lacking anything.
—James 1:4, NIV

In the file of one of my most recent letters of recommendation from a direct report, there is a sentence that blew me away. "Mrs. Johnson is a transformational leader." Wait. What? Maybe you will think me pathetic, but I have read that letter a total of five times in the past three weeks, simply so I can be reminded that someone who worked with me every day believed in my energy and motivation, stated that I engaged in the tough conversations every day, that my leadership was meaningful and inspiring, and that what I did in a school mattered.

Why do I need to see this? Survey results from all members don't say the same. Someone else's perspective would not state the same. With the day-to-day grind of living as a leader, you don't always get a chance to hear the impact you have on people.

Being dubbed a "transformational leader" is something I frankly did not expect.

Regardless of position, I do strive to live a life that transforms. What does a leader who transforms others look like? Feel free to look up the theory and read all about what the internet and scholars say about it, but I know it means that the person leading must be willing to transform themselves first and be intentional about leading their system. Something tells me the rest of you want a direct report to describe you this way as well, and if you don't want to transform people and systems, then what you really want to focus on is managerial aspects, right?

Here's a truth in our leadership journeys: Moments matter. Each one counts, and our ability to transform ourselves and those around us comes with the investment of painstaking daily choices to make each one matter. What follows are two highlighted examples of transformation from my own leadership journey. You will notice that neither of them came with an easy button. Neither of them show the process as easy or without pain, and you will also notice that each refuses to claim that the person experiencing the transformation is complete.

Transformation requires the ability to see the need to change, courage to venture into the process, patience in the pruning, and a commitment to ceaselessly strive for our best versions.

No, that would perpetuate a lie. Transformation requires the ability to see the need to change, courage to venture into the process, patience in the pruning, and a commitment to ceaselessly strive for our best versions.

Leaders Transform Themselves

Just when you thought there was no more that I could share about my own transformation, I've got a big one for you. So far, I have shared about growth in self-knowledge, values, intentions, and healthy views of titles. This transformation story is both lighter and deeper and has defined me in such complex ways over the past five years that I would be remiss if I did not share my running streak with you.

In my first year as an administrator, I was burning the candle at both ends. Fast. My energy was sustainable for that year, and I was running on passion and fulfillment from building relationships and living out my dream. Prior to admin meetings, I would listen to my supervisor and colleague talk about running, and I would internally scoff. Who seriously has time for that? Then I would begin making excuses for myself by comparison, like he was a dad and his last kid was older than my children who were three and one at the time. Exercise was for people with luxuries I did not have and "fringe hours," those before everyone else is up or down to bed where you can maximize time, a term not even on my radar. I would think about how my colleague's kids were out of the house, and she could go home and not even think about anything but her own needs. Each excuse gave me a reason to believe that my circumstances didn't allow me to take care of my own needs, and my martyring habits continued. The following year was not really any better, and I started to feel suffocated. My view of servant leadership as selfless, with any boundary setting being selfish, was becoming exhausting and morphing into depletion.

On Memorial Day weekend of 2014, I decided I needed some time to myself. Honestly, I was very unhappy when I started looking around my life and realizing how closed off it had become. I wasn't traveling anywhere to be with family due to stress and small children, and my husband was content to sit in the basement rather than be with me and my girls. A difficult time in our lives was on the horizon, uncovering how the routines of life were feeding discontent.

I started running as an escape.

Without any space in the world to be me outside of the various blessed roles, I was entering the dangerous territory of identity crisis I've already shared, and escaping was the motivation, though I didn't realize it then.

It felt so freeing to simply get out of the house and worry only about how much it hurt to run but felt so good for my soul. I ran and walked while I processed all the big feelings that had gotten stirred up. I describe the overall feelings as a complicated, tormenting vortex in that time. I ran hard. I ran to punish myself sometimes. That physical pain felt a lot better than the emotional anguish that had started with a period of false awakening and lies believing. *Ooph.* That was a tough spot.

On July 11, 2014, after spending a night away with my husband in one of our favorite locations, Duluth, Minnesota, I decided to submit my application for a position in a school six miles away. I didn't want to, but I knew to my core that I needed to do it, believing that proximity would solve much of our struggles with the battle between work and home. I clicked submit on the application just prior to the closing at midnight, and I have run every day since. Within that running streak spanning over five years at the publication of this book, lies the hard work involved in my personal, spiritual, and professional transformation.

In that first year in a new position, I ran from a lot—my marriage woes, my feelings of failure as a wife, mom, and friend, crushing stress at work, and the devastation of losing my brother to suicide. Each lace-up allowed me to retreat. Honestly, some of it was still escape, but it was also about holding onto something I could control. And it fueled me, fed me, started to refine me.

Eventually, I began running through it all—through the pain of loss and grief, through the challenge of restoration in my marriage, through the challenge of being labeled in alignment with my position and the cultural disruption occurring, through the uncertainty contained in so many circumstances of my life. And this *through* period lasted a long time, through marathon training, getting up at 4:00 a.m. and running along dark and dangerous streets, nearly tripping over deer carcasses, and listening to Stephen King as I ran with no fear. Maybe there was a period when I didn't care if I got hurt. "It would be doing something I love!" is what I would say to my husband and head out the door. In fact, I ran two marathons in this period, and they were wonderful experiences that taught me there was not much I couldn't face or conquer. Running for several hours straight every week and each day will make you feel that way, and I began to feel stronger in all spaces of my life, especially at work.

Finally, in the summer of 2017, I began running toward my best version. Forget the marathons. They were not my best. Though I was able to fit them in without adjusting my family's life too much, they were not fully with me in that season. My husband and girls were not there to cheer me on or celebrate at the finish line. It was sort of a life I was living separately, not my best version because it was not whole.

I will never forget the half marathon that changed it all in September 2017. When I forgot my earbuds and began really tuning in instead of zoning out, instead of moving into the numbing space where your mind floats away from that endorphin high, I tuned into my surroundings in a way I never had before. Looking at the gorgeous setting around me, I began to thank God for the beauty and my ability to run such a distance. I focused on the gratitude I felt for my sister traveling with me and bringing my niece and my girls so I could wave along the route, so they could see me accomplishing a really hard goal with laughter, a smile, and singing as I rounded the corner at mile ten. After a finish of less than two hours, a personal record and a first place for my age group, I focused on the gifts God had given me. Instead of the challenges of leading where I was, I began to see the mission of leadership more clearly, that it was me who was called to that space for a time of disruption in that learning community, and that I could use my gifts to continue growing us through it all. From that experience, I learned how it felt to focus fully on God's strength in me and the impact of that trust, and I used the feelings from that successful finish to translate to the remaining time I had in that learning community.

> I learned how it felt to focus fully on God's strength in me and the impact of that trust.

From that mindset, I could see how fortunate I was to be the principal at the expulsion table, loving the student still and being present in the spaces that were difficult. When it came to pushing hard for important change, my voice didn't waver as much, and I became less distracted by politics, more focused on our improvement plan. When climate challenges arose, I chose to lean into the conversations instead of away, speaking grace and truth as often as possible.

My running streak is not complete, nor is my transformation into my strongest leadership season. When we embrace the hard work, the daily steps, the lace-ups even on the days we don't want to, the conversations we would rather avoid, persevering in all circumstances, we most certainly transform ourselves.

One of my favorite extended analogies of this idea of personal transformation most recently came out in Jon Gordon's and Damon West's *The Coffee Bean*. We are all going to face challenges in our lives, whether they occur at home, at work, or in other spaces of our lives. A great way to think about how we handle the pressure is the analogy brought forth through the idea of items boiling in a pot. Where the boiling pot represents circumstances and challenge, the item represents us. Are we more like the carrot that, when placed in a pot of boiling water, becomes mushy and soft? Are we like the egg that transforms into a hardened version of itself? Or are we like the coffee bean that, when boiled, transforms the environment around it into delicious, energy-producing coffee?

When those fear giants in our lives loom, they bring with them pools of boiling water, and we need to determine how we will engage in the bubbling bath. When we choose to be a coffee bean, we have the power to transform the space in which we lead!

Leadership Transforms Systems

Over the course of a time of serving, the idea is to be able to see your mark somewhere in the fabric of your organization. Do not confuse this with a plaque or in image, but rather imagine an indelible mark of leadership that folds into the culture of the system and leaves a space for the next person to continue and mold. Transforming a system is not for the weak of heart, and meaningful change (the word nobody wants to use) comes with steady, well-paced, planned out, intentional drops at a time. You cannot bulldoze transformation. In fact, coming from someone who has been left to deal with the aftermath of that style, bulldozing is destruction, leaving a lot of work to build back. Of course, we know there are systems that need leveling. If you wish to rebuild, remold, and make meaningful and lasting change, you better be prepared for a lot of resistance, some sabotaging, and plan for standing in the minority at times. It is just a fact of change processes; however, once you get the ever-elusive critical mass on board to create the momentum, get after it! That is how we transform systems.

I've lead from various vantage points within systems, and there are many examples I would love to illustrate in this section. Some represent extreme ownership and others show where the lessons from failure were aplenty. What I want to illustrate in this section comes from my teacher leadership days. We must learn that transformation of systems does not happen with one person, and since this section is also about transcending titles, we should consider how we can all have an impact, regardless of title. In schools, given the right level of authority and distribution of leadership, teachers have great power to transform systems—together.

In my role as a "school improvement facilitator," I learned just how challenging school leadership and transforming a system can be. I worked in an exceptional system, full of rare and essential administrative and board support. We really were a family, full of loyalty, knowledge of one another, and dysfunction of course. Through a grant that I had co-written to receive federal funds to support important school improvement, we were working with an outside organization to implement comprehensive school reform. My role was to facilitate the process, recruiting and forming an "external study team" and creating a "building leadership team." Each team I was tasked with gathering included representatives from the greater community (external) and within the school (internal). Of course, I did this while also being a classroom teacher, so the role was really unique. We reviewed all the data available at the time, and I learned a lot about outside perspectives and community investments in a school. We examined data internally as the leadership team and, in the process, created a school leadership team that, while the structure has morphed, remains a decade later. They have refined the process and made it so much better as systems invested in positive change do. On this team, we developed a rotation for representation, processes for reviewing the data, norms for the team, goals, and systems for measuring our work. Through this team, much of the important work in a school stayed where it should: at the building level with strong investment from leaders with all titles.

I am proud to share that many members of the original team have either gone on to leadership roles in other districts and organizations or stayed in that organization and are leading there still. It is a true testament to the administration of that school, who distributed leadership and consistently influenced up in ways that allowed for dramatic system transformation. Our superintendent advocated hard for our rural community, the principal advocated for time and resources, and teachers advocated for what was best for students. We were doing professional learning communities long before the systems in which I recently served even thought to start them. And they continue to thrive, evolve, and innovate in that school.

We must be willing to have the tough conversations every day with clarity and grace in order to transform systems. We must bring others into the work. We must empower leaders in our organizations to carry out the transformations. And we must make ways to sustain the change. Otherwise, it is easy to just manage, but that's not the type of leader who transforms the environment around us.

Face the Fear

When you examine your own situation, are you willing to transform yourself? What areas most need attention? Are you a leader who seeks to transform systems?

Slay the Fear

Spend time reflecting about a transformation that your leadership has created. Document it in a similar way that I did and or commit to an intentional transformation.

Join the conversation and share your insights on social media.
#LeadwithFAITH

GATHERING STONES

- ***The Coffee Bean: A Simple Lesson to Create Positive Change*** by Jon Gordon and Damon West
- ***Starting a Movement: Building Culture from the Inside Out in Professional Learning Communities*** by Kenneth C. Williams and Tom Hierck
- ***Collaborative Leadership: Six Influences That Matter Most*** by Peter DeWitt
- ***Learning Transformed: 8 Keys to Designing Tomorrow's Schools, Today*** by Thomas C. Murray and Eric C. Sheninger

SECTION FIVE

Leading with Heart

Jesus replied: "Love the Lord your God with all your heart and with all your soul and with all your mind. This is the first and greatest commandment. And the second is like it: Love your neighbor as yourself."

—Matthew 22: 37–39, NIV

Leading with Heart Foundations

- Leading with heart means you must love people.
- Leading with heart involves wholehearted living and letting go of what weighs you down
- Leading with your heart means understanding how to notice and manage your own emotions as well as the emotions of those around you.
- Be the thermostat in a room and not the thermometer to lead with faith.
- Developing your emotional intelligence and the way in which you engage with those you lead creates trust and strong tethers.

I love people. Honestly love people. As an extrovert, I gain my energy from simply being around people, especially those whose light, passion, and exuberance for life mirror mine. I connect deeply with others and have always found a true sense of value in showing others my love through gifts, special notes, time together, laughter, and shared tears.

This can be problematic when you are a school leader, and it became one for me for a few reasons. One is that I have not operated well within a set of normed boundaries my whole life and have often found myself the object of other people's love in a way I never meant to initiate or reciprocate. In addition, pouring myself out to a classroom filled with students each day was very different from doing that to an entire school community. That level of pouring without getting filled back up in the right way (God's love) left me feeling depleted and confused.

Confusion ruled when I entered a chapter of my life when I felt little love back from a wide variety of spaces, but especially in my work environment. Not only did I not feel loved, I often felt disliked. I hate to admit that my human need to feel love from those with whom I worked and the lack of receiving that affection, left me feeling really weak—and very alone.

That time, however, also provided me with a mindset that has completely transformed every corner of my life. The experiences and what I gained from them will remain tethered to my heart for the remainder of my days.

With a broken heart, weakened spirit, and a false belief that I could carry it all, I had intermittent support, but no human could fill the void I had not even realized had begun to form. And no amount of human coping was helping. My friends couldn't do it. Work certainly wasn't doing it. My children were the closest, but I had removed myself from the center of their lives to make more room for their daddy because we had been struggling severely in our marriage, and I didn't have the stores he needed.

And God used all of that.

When I was at my lowest, and I was leaning into my vices, I got hurt over and over and over and over.

It took me a long time to realize that loving others was only going to get me so far in this life, and that filling my heart with love from flawed people would only result in flawed love. Loving people is the second command, but loving God was to be first and greatest!

I began to open my lonely and broken heart to be filled only by God. On my runs, where I had the space to be myself with nobody else's crushing expectations confusing my heart, I opened myself up to God's tender love and forgiveness. One run in particular, I asked Him to help me love only Him, to fall so deeply in love that it was all I yearned for, and this plea was so genuine and memorable that I can now vividly recall the stretch of road, the blades of grass blowing in the breeze to the rhythm of my footfalls. It was like time had stopped when I received a critical message, one that spanned way before that moment or the past few years, and the imagery remains vivid in my mind.

I was listening to music at the time, but not a playlist I had created. My iPhone was randomly shuffling through archived songs from my old iTunes account. Up popped a heavily rotated song from my past. With awe, I listened to Jars of Clay's "Love Song for a Savior," an old favorite with deep meaning. The image of a bird, a hummingbird in my mind, suddenly took on a new meaning. It was me, my spirit animal and the symbol woven throughout my life. From the lyrics burst forth an image of myself as that bird realizing that God is close to me in song and in heart, that he was calling to me, and I was running to him, praying the very prayer to fall in love with God which is contained in those lyrics. I could not believe how this plea aligned so deeply with my own life message in the moment, and seeing myself running and falling in my Creator's arms to say this very prayer is a moment I will never forget. My heart was pounding, and I was crying by the time I got home, so thankful for the feeling.

I spent many runs like that, just asking for God to help, believing He would, and still feeling empty outside of the run because I was holding back when the mundane nature of life's routines took over.

In August of 2017, everything began to change. It had been building. I could feel that the only thing holding me back from my pleas was me. I fell to my knees on the dock where I love to run to in my hometown, and I begged God to take my burdens and heal my heart to help me be strong. My plea included filling my weakness and removing any tether from me, and in my most vulnerable moment, I looked down to see a playing card. It was not remarkable, just the same old playing card we are all used to. When I flipped it face up, the image staring back at me was the king of hearts. Knowing that this was not a coincidence, I picked it up. I thanked God for the moment, as I stared in wonder at the card and made my way back home. God would be the King of my Heart. That morning, we went to church to worship, and it is no surprise that the song "King of My Heart" was playing. I had never heard it before, but the words were sung just exactly for me in that moment. From the connection to water and the playing card, my heart wept in wonder at the way God does show us that He is there when we need Him.

It is no small thing to be brave enough to see that these items are not coincidence and writing them down here is challenging to my core. They are so personal, but these clearly messaged moments signal a gateway for me. Before I began listening closely and carefully to the Holy Spirit and the direction for my life and documenting it on paper, these were the messages I received. I hear so many times from people that they want to hear God and how envious they are that I do and that He speaks so clearly to me. I offer this deeply personal example to show how it took my most desperate moments to genuinely seek this communication, to be brave enough to release my heart directly to God, and to see the messages He was sending through the means of communication that I would see and know. I needed to be courageous enough to see them—and to believe them.

An old popular song and a playing card could mean nothing to some people. To me, they meant everything and commenced a type of loving communication in its purest form. It is through my deep and unabashed love, and receiving it back, that I can love others better. I can show up at home, at work, in the tough times, through the frustrations, and love myself and love broken people. It is because my heart belongs first to the King of my heart, next to others, and through that clear line, I can lead with love.

Though it may not seem professional to some that I frame it this way, I very much love the staff, students, parents, and community with whom I have worked in my career as an educator. We don't use the word "love" a lot in professional settings, and we certainly need to be careful about it because there are so many variations of the word from noun to verb in our world. Still, the bare bones truth is that as a leader in a classroom and in a building, I have loved each and every person with whom I have worked. Not perfectly, of course, but love them I have. We may not say it, and we maybe should not say it, but we can sure show our love to those we lead, and I am willing to state in this work, that will never delete permanently once it is published, that loving others is one of our greatest calls as leaders. And if you cannot love those you lead—even those who challenge you, even those with whom you cannot agree, even those who are cruel to you, even those who show little love themselves—you are not leading with faith. Face it: You must love your people.

> *If you cannot love those you lead— even those who challenge you, even those with whom you cannot agree, even those who are cruel to you, even those who show little love themselves—you are not leading with faith.*

Do all the people with whom I have worked know that I love them? I wish I could tell you yes. Has it always been easy to love everyone? No way. How we express and receive love is complex, and there are many ways for our signals to get mixed up in the web of communication. Even though showing them love through following through on discipline was an act of great love, they still may not see it that way. Even though providing truth in feedback was showing love, they may not believe it was done in an act of love to help them improve. Even though going above and beyond, even when I didn't want to get out of bed with my own sadness some days, was an act of love, it still may not have been enough. Even though staying through the end of events to be sure kids had rides, chatting with families, and ensuring custodial crew were supported, at the sacrifice of time with my own children and sleep, may not have seemed like much or simply a given. Even though they may not ever see an act of service because a lot of leadership is giving credit to others, I still loved them.

That type of servant leadership (not martyrdom, remember) can feel thankless, unseen, and sometimes comes at a high cost of "ego." And it is risky because loving requires vulnerability. As a leader who loves their people and demonstrates it hundreds of times per day, you may never hear or see an appreciation for any of those caring acts. Your love may not be welcomed. Other days, you may receive it in spades. Loving those we serve means we do it anyway, regardless of reciprocation.

Here is the bottom line when it comes to leading with heart as a leader: *We don't love our people out of a desire to feel important.* The need to be needed is weakness and will never give you a full heart. Show up, serve, and remember that God loves you. And that will always be enough. Remind yourself of this truth often and refresh your stores daily with this truth at the base of your heart to keep it held up on the toughest of days.

> *Show up, serve, and remember that God loves you. And that will always be enough.*

Leading with heart can be challenging, and we need to walk all sorts of careful lines with how we show and receive love from those with whom we work in our professional lives. This section is not going to recreate ethics class for you. I am assuming a level of intelligence and reservation when it comes to this topic from my readers. I am also challenging you to be bold enough to lead with heart, even in the face of policy that may bind you, even in the midst of the most frustrating circumstances, and especially when you are working with the most unloved, be the leader who shows others what leading with love looks like. It is possible and exceptional to lead with heart without leaving your mind behind.

DAVID LED WITH HEART

David is known to be a man after God's own heart, and there are several references to David's heart in the Old Testament. The bottom line in this space is that no matter what David was doing, repenting after lust and murder, mourning the death of his child, friends, and family, celebrating in public, or on his death bed, David had a heart to praise God. It is not perfection that God sought from David and rewarded with a kingly legacy; it was the open and trusting heart that David offered to God in all circumstances.

Open my lips, Lord,
and my mouth will declare your praise.
You do not delight in sacrifice, or I would bring it;
you do not take pleasure in burnt offerings.
My sacrifice, O God, is a broken spirit;
a broken and contrite heart
you, God, will not despise.

—*Psalm 51: 15–17, NIV*

CHAPTER 12
Wholehearted Living

Most people need love and acceptance a lot more than they need advice.

—Bob Goff

Placement of this chapter worked out really well in the whole scheme of the FAITH acronym, because you have done a lot of introspective work before getting to this point in the book. Critical to being able to lead with love is honestly being able to know and love ourselves. If we do not come from a healthy space within ourselves, we cannot show love to others well, which can be very challenging for any of us. I am not saying that you have to be perfectly copacetic with every fiber of your being, but you do need to be able to have self-awareness and self-compassion, healthy boundaries, and a sense of balanced humility and authority as a leader to be able to love those you lead well. If you have done the work up to this point in all of these spaces, leading with heart is going to be an invigorating topic for you. If you are still stuck with the aforementioned preceding chapters, consider that growth through these areas may take time, but they are not going to simply happen. You must engage with these topics, so get to work, my friend!

If you are ready to launch into this topic, though, let's get right to the concept of leading with love. For cultivating wholehearted living, let's look to *The Gifts of Imperfection* by Brené Brown. From the thousands of research participants that she and her team studied, they gleaned many trends and key points from those who were living boldly, even in the aftermath of significant challenge. Here are the guideposts to live wholeheartedly.

Ten Guideposts for Wholehearted Living from *The Gifts of Imperfection* by Brené Brown:

1. **Cultivate authenticity.** Let go of what people think about you.
2. **Cultivate self-compassion.** Let go of perfectionism.
3. **Cultivate a resilient spirit.** Let go of numbing and powerlessness.
4. **Cultivate gratitude and joy.** Let go of scarcity.
5. **Cultivate intuition and trusting faith.** Let go of the need for certainty.
6. **Cultivate creativity.** Let go of comparison.
7. **Cultivate play and rest.** Let go of exhaustion as a status symbol and productivity as self-worth.
8. **Cultivate calm and stillness.** Let go of anxiety as a lifestyle.
9. **Cultivate meaningful work.** Let go of self-doubt and "supposed to."
10. **Cultivate laughter, song, and dance.** Let go of being cool and "always in control."

You will do yourself a disservice if you do not engage with Brown's work in this area, and the whole text which is grounded in her research on shame and resilience is beautifully woven together to create these guideposts. It is critical that you understand you can cultivate these in the best way you know how, and this section is going to provide you a few examples of how I have done so. You will notice that many of these guideposts have already shown up in previous chapters of this text.

For our purposes, I am going to share with you a few stories on cultivating these guideposts in the context of school. They are meant to simply invoke a belief in yourself that you are likely doing a lot of leading with heart already, but there are other ways you can cultivate more of it. Always more of the heart, my friends.

FAITH IN ACTION
NEIL GUPTA, DIRECTOR OF SECONDARY PROGRAMS, OHIO
@NEILGUPTA

It happened so fast that I know we didn't stop to consider all of the ramifications of the decision. Just the sheer potential in moving to a larger, suburban district with a greater role was enough for me to empathetically accept the job offer. Due to the continued support from my family, they agreed to the decision to leave our hometown and move to another city. While the distance wasn't far *per se*, we did leave behind our extended family, our church, and our familiar surroundings. In theory, it was the perfect time to move: I was feeling the itch for a change, my wife had just completed a degree in nursing and would be looking for a new job, and our oldest son would be starting middle school.

Although it was just an hour away from our hometown, the new city was a culture shock with the varied demographics and expectations. While I prided myself on meeting new people, establishing myself in a whole new city was like drinking from a firehouse. I dove into work, which consumed all parts of my day, thinking, and life. It took a few months for my wife to find a suitable job, and she was often lonely during the workday looking for friends to connect with. And my boys found it hard to integrate into the school community, searching for good friends to trust as they adjusted to their new life.

While I knew it was hard for them, and me, I downplayed the need for us to address the challenges early on. I kept telling myself it would get better on its own. Pretty soon, we discovered the need to lean on one another. Our bond as a family got tighter, as we realized the opportunity we had in talking with one another of things we were struggling with. My wife and I shared our struggles with the kids; it helped us to not only share what was in our heart but to also model the release just in talking. Our kids also felt a relief to be able to share about their anxieties, frustrations, and fears. Most often, we spent time just listening and giving one another a hug for comfort.

We also leaned on our church family. We found a great church early on, which seemed to offer connections for all of us to have with other families. Church members quickly took us in by praying with us and inviting us to dinners. Our oldest son plugged into youth group activities and was mentored by spiritual young men who became great supports for him.

It's been seven years since the move, and we still miss seeing our family on a regular basis. We also find ourselves in culture shock at times. But none of us regret the decision to move. It helped us to not only move to a place that provided us with more opportunities but it helped us to find the strength in leaning on one another to build our relationship as a tighter family. And we became even more aware of the need to pray, to seek out others to build community, to realize the true importance of family, and to step out in faith that things will get better.

+++

Cultivate Self-Compassion—Let Go of Perfectionism

Are you a right-brained achiever who must complete the task list for each day before you can fall asleep? Does the mess around you cause anxiety and lose the joy of moments while you pursue a clean and orderly environment? Do you get on yourself for mistakes or failures to the point of instituting penalties for yourself?

We buy too deeply into the lie that we have to be perfect and excel in it all, that there is no room for error, and that everyone else around us has it all figured out, so we can too. We fall into the comparison trap and think that we must be able to carry the load without a misstep, or we will be eaten alive, especially in leadership roles. To say nothing of large mistakes, we won't even allow little ones for ourselves. Sure, we can forgive our employees for falling short on deadlines, take the fall for errors when we delegate authority, but can never release responsibility. A humble leader does these things regularly and with grace.

But what about when we make the error?

If we are holding ourselves to the unattainable benchmark of perfection, we are really hypocritical. My educator readers certainly understand that formative assessments are in place

> *If we are holding ourselves to the unattainable benchmark of perfection, we are really hypocritical.*

in class and life to provide opportunity for growth and learning. Yet we expect ourselves to show up each day and meet expectations (or exceed) and feel worthless when we do not measure up perfectly. It's ridiculous, really. There is no such thing as perfection. No leader makes the right decision or hits the bullseye every single day in every way on all twenty-one components of the Danielson Model for Principal Effectiveness, or any other tool used to measure leadership effectiveness in an organization. We can strive for our best, but striving for perfection is a losing game.

To be clear, there is a difference between letting go of perfectionism and releasing expectations for excellence, professionalism, and strong leadership. If we cultivate self-compassion, it means that when we fall short of the mark, either provided to us or created in our minds, we are able to demonstrate just as much tolerance for the error, forgiveness, and allowance for correction that we would in our classrooms and with our staff. Though I have a series of examples I could share with you where I failed at perfection, this one I selected is from a time I am still recovering and grappling with in regard to guilt that remains. I want to give it to you because there was never a time in my life where I needed to demonstrate more self-compassion, but I never felt fully able to release the residue from it.

On December 2, 2014, I had in front of me a few weeks to complete rounds of formal observations of the entire staff in my building, which represented around thirty licensed staff members. We had a busy fall, and I had been saturated with the amount of time it had taken to learn this new system of evaluation, the quirky technology tied to it, and leading the district of principals new to it with onboarding and meetings. We were entering into the winter with stirring of turmoil, sustained more late turnover of staff prior to the school year start, and we were all brand new to our roles as administrators in the school. I was behind on my calendar plan and feeling significant pressure to meet not only the deadlines I had set but also the expectations from my supervisor.

I had woken up that morning not feeling very well, dizzy in fact. Taking the day off would have been wise, but I had an observation scheduled, and I did not want to miss it since the teacher had spent time preparing the lessons, and we had already met ahead about it. I recall the lesson from the day very well, and when I went back to my office to begin summarizing the teaching and learning I had observed, I saw my mom had called—a few times. This was not normal for her, so I closed my office door and gave her a call, a bit stressed, thinking I didn't have time to chat now and didn't want to forget to complete the arduous task of tagging evidence to standards for the observed staff member to review. Timeliness was key to this process. The trust in our building was tenuous at best, and I knew letting the teachers down in this process was key to avoid. But the news my mom had was the sort that stopped time and made me completely forget about that observation until a week later.

My brother had completed a suicide early that morning.

If you have ever experienced a personal tragedy in the midst of high-pressure life, you may be able to understand the impact of that sentence. I told my supervisor I would be back the next day as I had to complete the observations that were scheduled. It was not because of the mandates. It was because I knew how stressed out my teachers were. I would be back.

Friends, I didn't come back the next day. After somehow driving home and preparing a travel bag, trying to figure out how I would share this news with my husband and young children, school thoughts receded further away. I went to my husband's school at the end of the school day and gave him the news face-to-face. My pain was burning and fierce, sickening, as I related that my brother, my children's much-loved uncle, the dad of my husband's godchild, was gone. I went to my parents' house that night, which was two-and-a-half hours away, and we stayed up all night, reminiscing about our branch that had broken off, and the pain still radiates through my chest as I type this. We sat in disbelief, sadness, questioning, fear, and hollowness. I received one message from my supervisor, and I remember speaking with my secretary at the time, not wanting people to know what had happened. My heart was broken, and I didn't feel emotionally safe in that school at the time, to be honest. I didn't open up to any of them the way I could have.

When the funeral was over that weekend, I had delivered a eulogy for my big brother, and after we had finally shared the news with our daughters about their uncle, I returned to work. Then the stress caught up. And the depression covered me.

My brother died on December 2; his birthday was December 10. The anniversary of my cousin Julie's death was December 17. And then there was the family gathering for Christmas that announced his absence visually in a stunning way.

With all these triggers, I couldn't muster the desire to keep up the pace at work. I did it, but my heart was so broken, I didn't know how to process it all.

So I did forgive myself for missing deadlines, and I allowed myself to heal a little. Bit by bit. To say it was all healthy is completely false.

And I did complete all the observations and ridiculous amounts of paperwork that year.

But it was not done with perfect deadlines. I eventually forgave myself for that, but it took my staff a long time to bounce back. Missing deadlines as a leader reduces trust. Some maybe even never forgave me and simply wouldn't think to identity my life tragedy with an inability to function at the level of superhuman. Honestly, the expectation was foolish for culture anyway, but adding my pain to it was a recipe for failure.

Even through all of that, I did not give up. I completed the work. I gave myself compassion for not doing it perfectly timed. I simply committed to doing better each year. By the time I completed my fourth year with that system, and the disruption that distracted it a lot, I had more trust capital built, but it was a tedious, slow process.

Self-compassion paves the way for restoration.

The key is that I did not give up. I forgave myself for missing deadlines, and I persisted with my staff members, making sure they knew I cared about our work and about them.

We must learn that perfectionism is unattainable . Forgiving ourselves for our shortcomings is critical to leading wholeheartedly and to mending broken spaces within us. Self-compassion paves the way for restoration. I know this well and have lived to tell.

Cultivate a Resilient Spirit—Let Go of Numbing and Powerlessness

Listen, I have never once claimed perfection, and if I dare even skate the line of that persona, check me quickly. At the start of this text, I shared with you that my Enneagram results show a seven enthusiast. I alluded to issues with avoiding pain through unhealthy coping because the analysis of this style reveals that there is pain in our childhood we were conditioned to overcome at our healthiest and cover over at our most unhealthy.

I have lived in a period of fear and unhealthy coping, and, as I have already shared, there are times I wish could be simply erased from my history, but I am writing this text as a restored and redeemed, wholehearted leader with faith. So take my recent story about letting go of numbing as a gift to you readers with great heart from me.

Though it pains me to admit, I once went to school drunk with vodka in a clear container of Kool-Aid. Sorry, mom, dad, and educators. It was the seventh grade, and my need to numb was high. I was raised in a faithful home with parents who rarely imbibed. The strains of alcoholism ran deep in the belly of the family cave, and my parents were cautious about keeping us from alcohol. But they were also trusting parents who liked to travel, and I stayed home with my siblings when they were on vacation, and parties with alcohol happened. Sorry mom and dad.

I experienced a time that I know now was less experimentation and more numbing. Some topics are too sensitive for published material, so I simply state that there are wounds therapists can try to heal in us, but none was ever given the chance with me. God protected me through some challenging times, but I was definitely using other means to cope.

When I met my husband in 2000, I was at risk of the same. After a very dear friend had completed a suicide, I could have fallen again. I was in college, with parties everywhere, but there was a seeking in my soul for something better. Gracefully, God gave me Joe, who had strong moral values. He opposed alcohol and had disciplined habits and a stellar smile that I liked to smooch a lot. Because of Joe, I didn't touch alcohol for a significant portion of my young adult life. But I coped with the stress of life other ways, as a workaholic, a learnaholic, a readaholic.

In 2014, I picked up a wine habit enjoying social time with my work colleagues at the time. That habit hung on until the Holy Spirit convicted me to release it as part of my 2019 #SLAY goals. One glass of wine had morphed into buying bottles regularly by the case and "enjoying" a glass every night, even week days. It went from waiting until the girls were in bed to being a calming and delicious addition to dinner-making. Suddenly, I was receiving gifts of wine bottles and a Yeti wine holder at Christmas.

The truth is that I had started coping with the loss of my brother and a wounded marriage, as well as stress at work, and I continued the habit long after that was all gone. It clung to me. I would go a month without any alcohol to prove that I didn't need it. But in November and December, the most challenging time of year for me, I threw hard alcohol for martinis into the mix. I numbed myself this way consistently for four years before I realized I may have developed an issue. Even though I was listening to God and following my faith journey, I was still drinking wine most nights, numbing the sting of leaving my school, numbing the discomfort of the unknown.

Cultivating resilience, for me, meant letting go of the numbing completely for the entire 2019 year, and guess what? I have been more focused, more passionate, more successful, more able to manage stress. I've been better capable of processing my feelings, more apt to have a conversation with my husband about an issue, better able to sleep, more productive. Living this wholehearted way, aware of the numbing, has been a critical step in my faith journey, and cultivating this guidepost has been essential to providing deeper clarity and even more intention in this gap.

Be brave enough to let go of the numbing and cultivate a rise of your own. It may sting for a while. The bruises may be apparent, more visible to you, and the scars you see with clearer eyes may remind you of significant past hurts. Leaning into the spirit and cultivating your own resilient spirit will lead you to be battle ready in a way you could never be in a state of a numb stupor.

Cultivate Laughter, Song, and Dance—Let Go of Always Being in Control

More than ever, the safety of our schools and workplaces is a pervasive concern in our country. Aside from the social and emotional safety of those in our organizations, heavy-hitter items like mass shootings, threats, physical violence, and substance abuse preoccupy leaders' minds. As a leader, it is easy to get caught up in the need to feel like you are in control. This need to feel in control, and the constant barrage of issues, can lead a person to become very serious, to keep their guard up, and to lose the ability to laugh.

I have been a part of some intense investigations that have traumatized my heart. I have led through stressful scenarios steeped in uncertainty as we sorted through the details of threats and tragedies. Frankly, just thinking of these situations makes my back stiffen and heightens my protector valve to the highest notch. In the past month alone, two of my principal friends reported threat investigations that took the entire day, resulting in nothing, and we speak of it as though it is normal to receive a report of a gun in a backpack, false or not. The emotional and mental challenge school leaders face today is immense, and I am not overplaying this hand here; in fact, I have downplayed the reality of the day-to-day because we have all become just a bit desensitized to the fact that pervasive issues are inevitable in our learning communities across the country. My alter ego of a tough, leather-wearing defender remains intact today after building her over the course of the years, working alongside law enforcement to resolve concerns.

Living and working in these scenarios can harden a heart, but we must fight hard to keep the pliability in this vital organ to be able to lead well through trauma and in the midst of uncertainty. How can we possibly do this entrenched in the serious issues facing us as leaders? By cultivating laughter, song, and dance. And this is Brené Brown saying it, not me! And you know I just sang it, readers. You know I did.

We must remember that we cannot take ourselves too seriously. We can take our work seriously. We can take our mission seriously, and we can keep ourselves well in line with professionalism in a very serious way. Most of the time. But if we do not take time for laughter, song, and dance, we will miss the opportunity to flourish amidst our challenges. Allowing ourselves to let go of always being in control allows others to relax around us and builds relationships and memories, connections and bonds. Perfectly timed shared endorphin releases allow us to be human and wholehearted in a space much needed.

If we do not take time for laughter, song, and dance, we will miss the opportunity to flourish amidst our challenges.

How did I do this? Well, let's be honest: As I grew in my leadership journey, I learned how the absence of this cultivation or masking my actual propensity for laughter, song, and dance diminished my authenticity and put up walls that created barriers for trust. Friends, I need laughter. I need song. Dance is a bonus for me (but not necessarily those around me). I know an item that saved me when starting out in my most recent position—but having no literal clue what was about to go down in that district—was being a part (and the sole admin) of a retreat where staff rewrote lyrics to a mashup of 1980s songs. Okay, that is my heaven on earth, friends. I got up there and, after having met the staff that day, sang, "I love our school, so put another kid in the classroom, baby" at the mic. I had no clue what the refrain was to be and made it up on the fly. I distinctly remember thinking this was my place, my people. This is where I belonged with a crew of people who would laugh, sing, and dance together. Nothing that came after that day has diminished the experience of feeling like I belonged in that group in that moment, and I will forever remember seeing the others, who let loose rarely again in my presence, clapping to the beat and smiling. I saw those who grew together through adversity apart from me and came back by the time I left, those who watched from the sidelines and share their remembrance. I am so thankful that experience connected them to me and that I was willing to let go on day one. Later on, when I led out of fear, and when the weight of the world was on my shoulders, I still heard a staff member refer to me as Joan Jett a time or two and I could feel my heart beat.

Connecting experiences cannot be a one-off situation. Cultivating these guideposts means there is value in living each consistently. I am here to tell you that, though nothing in my leadership journey has been perfect, it is easy for me to see how the ability to incorporate laughter, song, and dance into my work environment as a teacher, a principal, and in my current work has not only impacted me in positive ways but those around me.

Here is a beautiful story from my lead administrative assistant, Kristin Tischer, to illustrate the point:

> "Three years ago, it was the best decision for our family for me to return to work, and I did so in a field and position I have never been a part of. I remember sitting in the high school conference room of a town I had never heard of before, interviewing with the principal, and being so nervous because I desperately needed this job to work out. From day one, Sarah has been not only an amazing boss but more importantly an amazing human. The personal connections we have made over the last three years have deeply impacted me. She's been there for my family, cheered me up when I needed it most, proven that people really do burst out into song and dance in real life, and been a source of sunshine on a few too many gloomy days. I have been blessed to work under her and will truly miss her as she moves on to a new chapter in her life."

Of all the items a person working with me directly could say, she homed in on the fact that I burst out in song and danced in real life. We shared space through many tense scenarios in our work together. Though I will never claim to have led perfectly, leading with heart and allowing my team to see the person behind the professional is one I am comfortable placing a premium on in this text. Allow yourself to be a blend of serious and sunshine. Your staff needs it.

Recently, I attended the graduation ceremony for my school after having been gone for a year but having poured my heart into the school for three years of the four with that class. What a perfect illustration of the impact of cultivating this guidepost when a student who approached me with a big hug and this gem: "The last time I saw you was at the lunch table when you sang "The Fresh Prince of Bel Aire" to me." Her brother, who was close by, laughed. "Yeah. That just doesn't happen. So cool."

I also remember the day of which she spoke. I remember how my heart was pounding after having finally gotten up on stage and singing in front of the school after "threatening" to do it for years, how I had not planned to do it but there were no formal acts signed up for what had become a yearly talent show. I was in classrooms that morning, soaking up the opportunity to be in the space one final day with these kids I loved and the staff I would miss, though I was trying not to show how much that affected me out of a desire to leave them strong. Just then, a student said, "I bet you are planning to surprise us and sing, Mrs. Johnson."

No way did I think they wanted that. No way did I think they cared about it.

Since there was evidence in front of me to suggest otherwise, I did it. My performance was not perfect, but it was bold and cultivated wholeheartedness in a way I will never forget.

Allow yourself to be a blend of serious and sunshine. Your staff needs it.

It turns out, they won't either.

I love this guidepost and will strive to cultivate it at home, work, and every area of life. The belief that we must always be in control separates us from being real.

It takes courage to lead with heart, but cutting through the fear is essential to leading others through these challenging times. Be bold enough to live the way you want to be remembered. Keep it light to be the light, friends.

Face the Fear

Are there any guideposts that feel particularly challenging to you in your current context? When it comes to vulnerability, are there barriers that create extra challenge for you to show up this way in your own life?

Slay the Fear

Select one guidepost and spend time in it. Think about what is that you specifically need to let go of in order to embrace the guidepost in your own life. Commit to intentionally building and cultivating this guidepost of wholehearted living.

Join the conversation and share your insights on social media.
#LeadwithFAITH

CHAPTER 13

Emotional Intelligence and Empathy

You never really understand a person until you consider things from his point of view . . . Until you climb inside of his skin and walk around in it.
—Harper Lee, To Kill a Mockingbird

Empathy—or the ability to understand others' feelings and needs—is also the foundation of a safe, caring, and inclusive learning climate.
—Dr. Michelle Borba

I vividly recall classroom experiences working with the classic tale *To Kill a Mockingbird*, where the storyline is woven intricately with motifs and themes that heavily emphasize empathy. The context in which Harper Lee both wrote the text and set it created myriad opportunities to learn and grow in the characters illustrated throughout the pages, as well as in the historical context tied to each setting. In classrooms and in school buildings all across the world, we have the opportunity to share wisdom and life-altering skills every day. Yes, mathematical principles are important and increasing literacy in all our students is essential, but developing emotional intelligence, and specifically empathy, is not only increasingly necessary but stands to impact lives forever.

To be an *affective* leader (one who incites positive change), we need to understand our own emotional intelligence capabilities and work to develop them. Additionally, we must ensure that we emphasize empathy.

Leading with faith is leading at our best, and according to Travis Bradberry, author of *Emotional Intelligence 2.0*, the research shows that 90 percent of top-performing leaders rank high in emotional intelligence, while only 20 percent of bottom performers are emotionally intelligent. The observation suggests that you can be a poor leader and still possess emotional intelligence, but the numbers are against you. In addition, they tell us that you are not likely to be a top leader without emotional intelligence.

> Leading with faith is leading at our best.

Let's dive further into emotional intelligence a bit as it relates to leadership qualities. Cultivating emotional intelligence, like much else in life, is personalized to your own needs, so let's look at it in four domains, which are defined in *Leadership 2.0* by Bradberry and Jean Greaves.

Self-awareness—The ability to accurately perceive your emotions in the moment and understand your tendencies across situations. (We spent a lot of time here in Section One of this text to help you with this domain.)

Self-management—Using awareness of your emotion to stay flexible and direct your behavior positively. This means managing your emotional reactions to situations and people.

Social awareness—The ability to accurately pick up on other people's emotions and understand what is really going on with them.

Relationship management—Using awareness of your emotions and those of others to manage interactions successfully.

As you consider these four domains, it is important to understand that each of us are strong in particular areas, and the key is to grow them all as leaders. Of course, if we cannot regulate ourselves, it seems that it would be nearly impossible to manage others, so if you are struggling with this self-awareness and regulation, that sounds like the perfect place to start.

Regulating versus Gauging

One of my favorite analogies when I think about a highly emotional intelligent leader is one who can be a thermostat, not merely a thermometer. I first heard of this analogy during a particularly challenging time in my own life and leadership during a sermon at church. In it, our pastor at the time blew my mind open with this simple analogy that relates to so many aspects of school leadership. I realized one of the largest sources of frustration at the time was feeling like the temperature of our school climate was running really hot or frigid with little regulation, and the consistent feeling of instability was leaving me drained. It occurred to me at that time that I needed to install new batteries into my own thermostat and get to work on regulating!

When it comes to taking this analogy deeper into the emotional intelligence domains, we can understand that there is a role for gauging both the temperature of yourself and a room. Awareness is critical to effectively understand what is happening within yourself and in your surroundings, but simply marking the temperature is only half the equation. The strongest leaders can set the temperature for themselves, as well as that of a space, and adjust when the air gets too hot or too cold. Thermostats are regulators, and they keep the temperature in a room at a desired level.

Think about this concept for a minute in relation to your own context. When you place the concept of thermometer, are you able to read your own temperature? Are you able to walk into a room and feel the tension points or know when all is well and thriving in a room? The trouble with stopping here in your emotional intelligence journey is that if this is where your skills end, you will not be able to lead and influence when it matters most. Consider a scenario where you are in the midst of a conflict that continues to escalate. If all you are able to do is gauge the temperature and not regulate, it is likely that your own temperature will rise with that of the hostile person. Say an angry parent ratchets up to the point of yelling. Without the ability to regulate both yourself and the other person, you will likely spout something out of your lips for which you will later have to apologize or for which you can be reprimanded. Nobody wins when a leader loses his or her cool.

We must always remember that people are in a state of high emotion for a reason. Their actions may have little to do with us, and much to do with something else going on. A thermostat leader can look beyond the moment and seek to understand what might really be affecting the other person. Hence, relationship management is thermostat behavior.

In that same scenario, consider how regulating your own emotions in order to then regulate the temperature of the conversation can have significant impact. If you remain at a comfortable 65 degrees, speaking calmly, listening, using language that distills and remain curious without engaging in the rise, you are regulating and winning. This is not saying that you remain aloof to the point of being rude or disengaged. It means that when the temperature rises, you remain steady and calm it down a notch or two.

Look, I know this is not easy, but when we consider how emotional intelligence plays into our core values, I would bet my firstborn on the fact that each of you has something along the lines of trust, relationships, and connections. Maintaining composure during someone else's meltdown will make you a winner every time. You will be living in your values and demonstrating emotional genius!

> *Maintaining composure during someone else's meltdown will make you a winner every time.*

You may be thinking right this minute about a thermometer moment where the mercury spewed out the top of the shattered glass on your gauge or cracked from the frigid temps. Not one of us are perfect at this every time. The key is to continually work to develop these skills by way of practice, experience, and mindfulness in the moment. Instead of thinking of your failures, I encourage you to take a moment and call up a success in this area, even if you have to dig deeply. Most often, we may not recall the successful moments because they are not emblazoned in our memory due to shame or embarrassment. The moment was handled well and diffused. This is what strong leaders do all the time. Just be sure that you call up an example in your own life to reflect upon.

One of the most successful examples I can think of in maintaining my cool was an angry parent—and I mean a hopping, cussing, finger-pointing, name-calling, threatening-to-get-a-lawyer-and-get-me-fired parent. This person hated me for crimes I had no idea I had even committed, and maybe it was simply because I was breathing. There was nothing I could do to calm this person who was in a fit of irrational behavior, and I recall after the fact getting advice that I should have yelled back. That was terrible advice. In the face of this parent's anger, I held my boundaries and kept my calm. I listened while the individual called me names and insulted me over and over for my decisions. They shared how the only smart person they ever had in my chair was two principals ago, and I knew nothing about this school and its people. With each blow, I remained in my chair and calmly asked for more clarity, gently reminding the individual of where we were and the expectations. I asked if we should continue the conversation when "we" were calmer and redirected and set boundaries when name-calling started.

I will never forget how my heart was racing, and I had to hold my hands in my lap, how each terrible word I was called or each line about how I was not good enough made me want to scream.

Yet I didn't.

I will never forget how the individual ended by saying, "I will pray for your soul," before leaving the office and cussing on the way out.

I had many more opportunities to remain calm with this same parent over the course of the years. Eventually, I mediated meetings with teachers and this parent. Somehow, this parent and I became allies at the end. Somehow, this parent told me I shouldn't be leaving when I moved on from that learning community. An update from this parent recently revealed: "I learned a lot, and I don't come in hot anymore."

We always have an opportunity to influence, and one of the most impactful ways we do that is to be a thermostat, even in the hottest of conditions.

FAITH IN ACTION
BETHANY HILL, EDUCATOR-ARKANSAS-@BETHHILL2829

We experience a multitude of feelings on a daily basis. Things happen around us that push us into an emotional state, even if others don't notice. We move in and out of various emotions throughout the day, and sometimes even in our dreams. Our emotions will help us connect with others, or withdraw completely. People address their emotions in different ways, some being easy to read, and others being more difficult. Empathy is at the heart of every emotion. When we seek to understand the feelings of others, we are investing in lives. It is the key to open the hearts of others, and sometimes our own hearts.

When I think of my childhood, one of the first people who come to mind is Fred Rogers from Mr. Rogers' Neighborhood. He was so happy, and always calm. Even when people and characters around him were upset, his voice remained soothing, gentle, and full of wisdom. He reminded me that I was a child, even though I experienced adult situations and was growing up faster than I should. Mister Rogers had this way of making me feel so important, and he spoke directly to my heart through the television. He always knew what I was feeling, and because of that, he was my hero. Mister Rogers mastered empathy. He lived it daily through his ministry and advocating for children.

When I was a little girl and first began school, I had separation anxiety. School was this structured place that was opposite of my world. I cried for weeks each morning my mother left me, and remember vividly the extreme nature of the meltdowns. My teacher could have easily sent me out of the classroom for the counselor or someone else to handle, but she didn't. Each morning, she gave me a hug, gave me space, and time to find my calm. She never told me to "calm down", not even once. I remember her voice being so soft, and it was never harsh or loud. The only other people in my life like this, were my mother, and Mister Rogers on the television. They all three had this ability to bring the calm during my storms. Looking back, I know that empathy is what they offered me.

Empathetic people are not looking to fix us. They are looking to listen and understand us. Although it requires a level of vulnerability, allowing others to empathize with our circumstances is healthy and healing. I refer to empathy as this amazing super power that provides a force to be reckoned with. It is directly linked to human connection and seeking peace.

I sometimes wonder how my schooling would have been different had I not spent my first year with a loving and empathetic teacher who wanted to know me--all of me. She wanted to know the great things, and the not so great things. She saw something in me when I only saw a weak little girl in handmade clothing, not knowing if she could be accepted. When I see children at school who are anxious or exhibit extreme behaviors, I immediately connect. I was that child once, and I know that what they need is patience, understanding, listening, and love. That is what empathy is all about.

+++

Leading with heart means you believe in the power of emotional intelligence and seek to cultivate your own, as well as the emotional intelligence of the staff at your school and the students in your building. With Dr. Michelle Borba's recent research stating that our teens are 40 percent less empathetic than they were three decades ago, we know it is important to focus on social-emotional learning. The good news is that we can! First, knowledge is power. Let's explore empathy a bit.

Empathy is a teachable skill and one that has the ability to impact our daily lives and literally the entire world. When we are empathetic with others, we show love in the form of compassion because we understand others' feelings and needs. As leaders with heart, it is essential for us to build our empathy skills so we can make deeper connections with those we serve and so that we can ensure our learning environments and work spaces are safe and inclusive. In Dr. Michelle Borba's book *Unselfie: Why Empathetic Kids Succeed in Our All-About-Me World*, she identifies nine principles for empathy that can be taught. Diving deeper into these will be an asset for the work you do in your school, and a bonus is you can build your own empathy skills by learning in any of these areas yourself!

1. Emotional Literacy
2. Moral Identity
3. Perspective
4. Moral Imagination
5. Self-Regulation
6. Practicing Kindness
7. Collaboration
8. Moral Courage
9. Growing Changemakers

In addition to these principles, we cannot just implement a kindness day and walk away, people! Below is a list from Borba that help us think about making this learning meaningful. For a gut check and validation for why we need to lead with faith, check out number seven on her list.

Principles of Effective Empathy Education

Effective empathy education requires seven core principles, guided by strong, empathetic school leaders.

1. Ongoing: Educating for empathy is not a one-time lesson, but a continual focus.
2. Woven-In: Empathy competencies are integrated into content and interactions, not tacked on.
3. Meaningful: Instruction is authentic, touches the heart and mind, and stretches "me" to "we."

4. Internalized: The goal is for students to adopt empathy competencies as lifelong habits.
5. Student-Centered: Students' needs, not curriculum, drive the lessons and experiences.
6. Respectful Relationships: Empathy breeds in a culture of respect and caring.
7. Empathic Leadership: Empathy is modeled, expected, and core to a principal's vision, purpose, style, and interactions.

If you are a person who struggles with empathy in your own life, the good news is that unless you are a sociopath, you can teach yourself to be empathetic, just like we can teach our students and influence our staff.

Facing the Fear

When considering emotional intelligence domains, and empathy specifically, is there anything that makes you uncomfortable? With the idea of thermostat versus thermometer, which pieces resonate with you and your context?

Slay the Fear

Spend time in self-reflection in regard to emotional intelligence and empathy. How strong are you in each domain, and which areas do you need to cultivate to strengthen your EQ? Make a plan to build your skills in the area you identified.

Join the conversation and share your insights on social media.
#LeadwithFAITH

GATHERING STONES

- ***The Gifts of Imperfection: Let Go of Who You Think You're Supposed to Be and Embrace Who You Are*** by Brené Brown
- ***Unselfie: Why Empathetic Kids Succeed in Our All-About-Me World*** by Dr. Michelle Borba
- ***Leadership 2.0*** by Travis Bradberry and Jean Greaves

CONCLUSION

Rise Up from the Pit

It has always seemed to me that broken things, just like broken people, get used more; it's probably because God has more pieces to work with.
—Bob Goff

We are never defeated, not even when all the evidence appears to the contrary. If you are still breathing, there is always tomorrow, and it can always be new.
You don't have to be who you were.
—Jen Hatmaker, Of Mess and Moxie

Living in my own pit of fear felt like existing in a multiverse where my own personal hell consisted of watching the events of my life occur on two parallel screens. One version featured me skipping around the world, waxy and shining, radiantly trying to save the world around me and facing each new challenge that seemed to come at me from every angle. Fear entangled itself into the fibers of my clothes, creating an illusion of control on the outside but a deep hollow in my stomach and heart. The other version suffered in the cell I had created at the very bottom of the pit where I lay dried up, filthy, stained, and chained on a heap of ashes—thirsty, bloodied, and broken.

Scariest from that time is that shiny version didn't know chained version existed, and little miss cinder girl was too broken to cry for help.

Until it was time to #RISE.

FAITH IN ACTION
TIM CAVEY, MED, EDUCATOR, HOST OF TEACHERS ON FIRE PODCAST, BRITISH COLUMBIA, @MISTERCAVEY

"Come home quick. The house is on fire!"

The date was December 3, 2012. There was an hour of classes left in the school day, but this was the text message I saw on my phone. It was my landlord, and she wasn't kidding. With obvious concern, I excused myself from the building as soon as possible and took the train home to my basement suite.

When I arrived, fire trucks and crews blocked the street, and fire inspectors were wrapping up their work. An hour earlier, to make sure I wasn't sleeping through the fire in my suite, they had smashed through my door. My living space was sitting in an inch of water from the fire hoses, but that was nothing compared to the damage the fire had inflicted on the main and upper floors of the house. The structure was a complete loss.

Stunned, I tried to take in this rapid change in circumstances. I was suddenly homeless, and with no family in the immediate area, it would be up to me to find a new place to live. To complicate matters, I was working through a divorce at the time, a slow extrication from a dysfunctional relationship that had led me to this city in the first place.

My life isn't supposed to look like this, I thought.

Thankfully, God answered my prayers for a new place to live with incredible speed. Within twenty-four hours and following a few minor miracles, I was able to move into another fully furnished basement suite that was even closer to the school where I taught. Even while moving my belongings into a rental van on a dark and rainy December evening, I felt the warm embrace of a caring Father. All was not lost.

My living situation was resolved for the time being, but my life's path forward remained uncertain. What was my purpose? Where was God calling me to live? With the wreckage of a dysfunctional marriage in my wake, and as I struggled with the stigma of divorce, how could I possibly contribute anything of value to the lives of others again?

Over the days, weeks, and months that followed, I gradually unwound from the emotional fetal position and social isolation that had gripped me since separation a couple of years prior. First, I leaned into the support of loving colleagues, finally sharing with transparency and asking for support when needed. I visited local churches, first attending anonymously and then plugging into small groups. I formed new relationships with other believers, continuing a journey of emotional and spiritual healing. I learned to fully embrace the grace of Christ, rejecting the shame of marital failure, and instead learning to empathize more deeply with others facing similar challenges. I was learning to breathe again, and as that process of recovery continued, I slowly regained the capacity to love and serve others in meaningful ways.

Fast forward to 2019, and God has rewritten my story in ways that are nothing short of miraculous. I am married to a beautiful woman whose heart beats for Jesus and whose love fills me with a joy I never thought possible. I am a proud stepdad to two handsome boys, and the three of us drive to a wonderful school campus together each day. My family attends a vibrant church plant community in the neighborhood, and we are privileged to host a life group in a beautiful home of our own. A single mom and her son even call our basement suite home.

As I sit in my home office typing these words, I think back to that dark and rainy night back in December 2012. Standing in the ashes of a dark and burned-out house, I was surrounded by feelings of failure and loss. At the time, it was hard to imagine a future with any sort of light or promise, yet my Heavenly Father saw a path forward. In Isaiah 61, we read of His longing to exchange ashes for beauty, mourning for joy, praise for despair. This was my experience, and this is the heart of our God.

+++

People often ask me how I began discerning the voice of the Holy Spirit in my life. The literal truth is that my awareness started with a gradual realization akin to the sensation I imagine when a person comes out of a deep coma. I slowly realized the close and soothing whisper in my ear was also the one slicing my heart between my shoulder blades, and I began to strain toward the distant call that had been echoing through watery ears. When we are in the pit, we must listen for the distant call, the one whose echo travels through the light and shines the way back out.

The difference between that once distant call and the now distant whisper is as discernible to me as light and dark. Staying close to that call and seeking that voice above any other is how I hear. In order to hear, we must first listen. I am grateful every day for the chance to listen, and I choose to take the opportunity so that the slicing whisper will not ever gain on me again.

> *In order to hear, we must first listen.*

Hoisting myself out of that pit required a lot of work, but I am forever grateful for the process of it all.

My struggle led me into one of the most courageous and fulfilled chapters of my life so far. In this season of slaying giants, I am bold enough to believe that my own framework to rise up is worthy. It is not research based; it is life based. My framework comes from a mix of my own clawing up, the grace of wisdom directly from my spiritual maturity, study, and collections of lessons throughout my life from wise mentors, as well as painful lessons from those who have sought to hurt me. My deepest desire is for you to use this framework in your own life to rise out of the pit of fear and into the radiant shine of courageous faith.

Rely upon trusted mentors and experience but retain your own mind.

Interrogate. Become a relentless investigator of the facts, separating lies from truth.

Seek answers, forgiveness, and silence.

Expect to be healed.

Understand what tripped you into the pit.

Prepare to face fear giants again.

Rely upon wise mentors who not only hold your best interests at heart but are willing to speak truth and grace to you. If you are messing up, they are the ones who will be honest. Our falls into the pit are all unique, and that journey of retracing our steps quite individualized, so when I say that you need to retain your own mind through it, just be sure that your mind is sound and not driven by lies. If your thoughts are on shaky ground and informed by fear, it is harder to rely upon your own mind. For me, I have learned to use this filter for those I rely upon for good counsel.

Trust—They have shown themselves to be of the utmost in integrity, forming my inner circle, and can keep whatever I tell them tight to where it needs to stay.

Wise—They have experience and gained lessons over their lives in the topic I am relying upon them for and they aren't quick to advise, but seek to listen and help me discern.

Love—I have learned that when someone loves us, they show it through giving us grace and truth. If we are acting foolishly, they will tell us. They will also offer us the grace of forgiveness for our lapses.

Faith—My filter here is related to alignment with grace-filled truths, not rules, but any advice they give me must be guided by a strong faith.

Going it alone in the pit is a huge mistake. All you will do is fall further into the depths and gradually lose pieces of yourself. Isolation will only exacerbate the issues you are facing. Reach out to start climbing up.

Interrogate. Be absolutely relentless in uncovering the facts of the situation. The very real enemy seeks to steal, kill, and destroy (John 10:10). The easiest way to do that is through deceit, and it is way too easy for us to buy those lies. The ultimate impostor makes us believe we are not worthy and shackles us in fear that our mistake is too egregious to be forgiven or corrected. If we are not tireless in examining each lie, each piece of the puzzle, each narrative we

> *Isolation will only exacerbate the issues you are facing. Reach out to start climbing up.*

began rewriting, we will lose ourselves in the muddy mystery of an unsolved case. Pierce the darkness of the interrogation room with that bright light, and allow yourself to question the lies you have been creating and believing.

When we are in the pit, this one can be so hard to discern. I once believed the presence of a hummingbird, my lifelong "spirit animal," was a sign that I was to seek life away from my husband and my home. Nothing could have been more wretchedly deceitful, and it pains me to consider that I was not careful about examining what I was seeing as false. Deceiving ourselves can be easy if we are not constantly taking ourselves through the entire case file. That is not to say we should overthink the lies. It is to say that we should be looking at whatever story we have created to examine for fact or fiction. For me, going to Scripture and core values always helps me pull back the veil.

Seek whatever it is that you need to begin the climb out of the pit. For some, this can be answers to understand a major hurt, and for others this may be forgiveness. For all of us, it is silence. When I was in the pit years, I avoided silence because I was afraid of the pain that was lurking there. On my runs, I would listen to music, audiobooks, podcasts. Instead of facing the reality of the shattered pieces that lay strewn at my feet as I pounded the pavement to run away, I drowned the truths their crunch cadence was trying to whisper to my heart. I vividly recall the months after my brother died, avoiding silence because I was so afraid of the images my mind would conjure of his last moments. Instead of healing and facing the wretched reality, I avoided it by keeping noisy and busy. If I was too still, I might think of all the parts of my life that were out of order and actually face the discontentment and pain from hurts.

When I chose silence, forgiveness came. Answers started to unfold and, to this day, I continually seek the stillness and reflection that accompanies the silence. It is in seeking this light that we can be sure to stay away from the shadows that threaten to trip us and pull us back into that pit.

Expect to be healed, restored, redeemed. When I think of this piece, I recall watching both of my daughters persevere to reach the top of the rock-climbing wall. At some point, they needed to believe and expect that they would hit the bell at the top. If we are coming out of the pit, we must expect we will reach the light where we will be healed and restored. When we follow the RISE UP framework, we have nothing else but to expect this for our lives. Our emaciated souls can refresh in the open air and light once we are able to come out into clarity. Bring your fears and sorrows, pain, and dry heart to the light, and expect to radiate life once again.

Understand what tripped you into the pit. This step requires much humility, seeing facts clearly, and a willingness to own your role in the tumble. Interestingly, I have learned that when I look to others for where I tripped, I know I never have the real answer. Others can hurt us, yes. But we are the ones who allow ourselves to fall into fear for a wide range of reasons, and mine for most of my life goes back to that core style Enneagram seven. When I avoid pain, either by not facing directly those who have hurt me or numbing an ache, I begin to live outside my values and fall to fear. Over the span of my life, I can see patterns the enemy constantly uses to trip me up. Once we understand where we fell in the first place, we can work hard to avoid the same trap. Once we catch hold of that pattern in our lives, we will be empowered to take giant leaps past the holes on our own path.

Prepare to face fear giants again. Critical to leading with courage is never forgetting to expect more giants to appear in our view on any terrain. When we look at rising out of the pit as releasing ourselves from chains placed by the enemy to keep us down and claiming our faith publicly, we can bet there will be a double down of efforts to pull us back in. We will be faced with fear arrows and lie slingshots. If we come out of the darkness expecting to be chased, we can run that race with endurance, and we must. One of the greatest lessons in my own rise and leap is that the giants came after all the hard work of rising. The good news is that every new skill we gain in preparation outside of the battle will make us capable of slaying our fears each time they present. A real tangible way to prepare? The entirety of this text is a start. We must equip ourselves by courageously leading with FAITH once again. And again.

Slaying Takes FAITH

Faith is not believing in my own unshakable belief.
Faith is believing an unshakable God when everything in me trembles and quakes.

—Beth Moore

By now you understand the FAITH framework and what it means to lead through your fears. We have taken this journey together, and I have shared with you a portion of my own fears, failures, and triumphs. I've given you others from the field who are working on their leadership journeys, and I've done my best to provide you resources and prompt your thinking in regard to how you can apply this framework in your own life. None of us are going to be perfect at courageous leadership. What I have come to understand and deeply believe is the bottom line in my own life is slaying takes faith, not just FAITH.

David shows us what it takes to really slay fear. If you read the stories of David before and after he was a king, you will know that Goliath was not the last opponent he would face. We hear so much about the encounter, probably because of the confidence David exuded, the against-all-odds victory. Unless we study, we may not know about how David was anointed long before he battled Goliath, though he was not the titled "firstborn" and was, in fact, overlooked until Samuel received a spiritual prompting to look further into Jesse's line. We see how after that anointing, David remained in a low status as a shepherd. It was in that role that he honed his leadership, care, and courage skills with the animals he tended. We see how his brothers were soldiers in the war but not him, and he was on a humble servant leader's mission to bring food to his brothers when he first heard of the terror Goliath was causing to Saul and the others. We see how he was offered the king's armor before going into battle, but denied it knowing he had been trained well and called through God's strength to the battle, and that alone would suffice. We see eventually how David's favor with God, confidence, and light were a source of jealousy from King Saul, who sought to snuff it out as David rose in life. Like David, none of our stories end at the epic battle scene. When we trust and continue on a faith journey, we will encounter many new challenges meant to grow us.

Just like David, a call to leadership means always more giants to slay in the future. David battled giants throughout his life, including his own sin, including adultery and murder with subsequent loss of a child, and persecution from Saul. Even so, David led with FAITH through every fear and in every battle until his own end, giving his heart to God despite the many pits he fell into throughout his life.

David led freely as himself, even worshipping in a way that embarrassed his wife. He always knew his purpose, battling back the desire to build a temple and leaving it to his son. David was intentional about making space for God in his life, praying even in the midst of mourning. He didn't get caught up in titles; though he was anointed to be king, he still gave Saul much reverence even after he was dead. David is known thousands of years later, not for the ways he failed, but the way he led with his heart, loving others and praising God in all circumstances. Because David led with FAITH, we still know his story today and can look to his victories as proof that no giant is too big, no sin too unredeemable, no role too lofty, no trial too lengthy and fearful for us to overcome.

It is encouraging to consider that with our own focus on foundations, we too can rise up anew and slay each new fear giant.

We simply need to build foundations to rise up and bravely, relentlessly lead with faith.

BIBLIOGRAPHY

My Faith Story

Bessey, Sarah. *Out of Sorts: Making Peace with an Evolving Faith.* New York: Howard Books, 2015.

Evans, Rachel Held. *Inspired: Slaying Giants, Walking on Water, and Loving the Bible Again.* Nashville: Nelson Books, 2018.

From Rising to Slaying

Brown, Brené. *The Gifts of Imperfection.* Center City, MN: Hazelden Publishing, 2010.

Taylor, Barbara Brown. *Holy Envy: Finding God in the Faith of Others.* San Francisco: Harper One, 2019.

Chapter Four

Achor, Shawn. *The Happiness Advantage.* London: Virgin Publishing, 2011.

Niemiec, Ryan. "What Do We Know About Signature Strengths?" *Positive Psychology News.* April 28, 2015. Accessed September 19, 2019. positivepsychologynews.com/news/ryan-niemiec/2015042831514.

Chapter Five

Brown, Brené. *Dare to Lead.* New York: Random House, 2018.

Chapter Six

Angelou, Maya. Twitter post. August 19, 2015. 2:18 p.m. twitter.com/drmayaangelou/status/634112210143350784?lang=en

Chapter Seven

Covey, Stephen. *The Seven Habits of Highly Effective People.* New York: Simon & Shuster, 2013.

Chapter Eight

Covey, Stephen. *The Seven Habits of Highly Effective People.* New York: Simon & Shuster, 2013.

Zomorodi, Manoush. *Bored and Brilliant.* New York: St. Martin's Press, 2017.

Chapter Nine

Mielke, Chase. "Is Teaching Worth It?" YouTube video, 5:03. Posted October 2015. youtube.com/watch?v=bySSgjbjqqw.

Achor, Shawn. "The Happiness Advantage." TedTalk, TedX Bloomington, 12:05. ted.com/talks/shawn_achor_the_happy_secret_to_better_work.

Chapman, Gary. *The Five Love Languages: The Secret to Love That Lasts.* Chicago: Moody, 2015.

Chapter Eleven

Gordon, John and Damon West. *The Coffee Bean.* New York: Wiley, 2019.

Chapter Twelve

Brown, Brené. *The Gifts of Imperfection.* Center City, MN: Hazelden Publishing, 2010.

Chapter Thirteen

Borba, Michelle. *Unselfie: Why Empathetic Kids Succeed in Our All-About-Me World*. New York: Touchstone, 2016.

Bradberry, Travis and Jean Greaves. *Emotional Intelligence 2.0*. San Diego: Talent Smart, 2009.

Bradberry, Travis and Jean Greaves. *Leadership 2.0*. San Diego: Talent Smart, 2012.

ACKNOWLEDGMENTS

A project such as this text does not happen without support and encouragement from many important people.

Thank you to my parents who did the hard work of growing my faith foundations from an early age. Without your dedicated, loving guidance for a literal lifetime, my rise and leap could not be so courageously taken.

Thank you to my husband, Joe, for your steady foundation to create conditions where I could travel this journey in faith and trust. Only crazy people leave a job without one lined up, right? What a gift your willingness to risk much alongside me has been!

Thank you to my incredibly brave daughters, Selene and Adelle. The space between leaving what was known and living fully intentioned on God's path has yielded the most blessed year of our lives.

Thank you for believing your mother can do anything, drawing pictures and cards with sunrises to remind me, and unwaveringly supporting your mama.

Thank you to my nest crew—my siblings—who have somehow managed to gift me a lifetime of pain and promise and remain some of my favorite people on the planet. I am so glad God gave you to me as well as your special children and all the branches we have created on this fun-loving, laughter-filled family tree.

To my incredible colleagues who took a leap of faith to lead with faith with me and contribute to this message as well as endorse it boldly, I am extremely thankful. Some of you I have never even hugged in real life, yet you continue to support and encourage this journey in ways that astonish me. Each of you grows me, pushes me, and emboldens me to believe that there is a mission in my message too.

To my professional learning community who continues to wrap arms lovingly around me with each obedient step, especially my WISE Women, I am so fortunate to do life in each new space with all of you--too many to name--what a blessing!

To my publisher, Erin Casey, thank you for believing in this real faith, real-life story and for creating space at the table for this message. Your wisdom, perseverance, and your own light mean a great deal to me, and I am grateful that you would share this message with the world.

Finally, to the staff, students, parents, and communities with whom I have had the absolute honor to learn with over the years, thank you for blessing me in ways I would never have fathomed as a teacher or administrator in your midst. Each learning community remains rooted deeply with love inside the depths of my heart forever. Each one has blessed me with the cherished lessons contained in this text and so many more remaining to be discovered and regifted. You have been a passionate focus of my adult life, and I love you all. Yes, even those of you who like Neil Diamond. I can't help myself. It is all of you in these schools who have helped me become the version of me that I am today as a leader, and I will seek to honor your contributions to my own life journey as I continuously seek to lead with ever more faith.

BRING SARAH JOHNSON TO YOUR ORGANIZATION OR EVENT!

Sarah provides high-energy, engaging, interactive, inspiring, and impactful keynotes and workshops that will leave participants more centered and empowered to lead well at work, home, and life.

The sessions below can be presented as keynote or breakout sessions or extended into half or full-day workshops to transform lives.

- *Lead with FAITH—Firm Foundations to Empower You to Slay Fear and Lead with Courage*
- *Lead Free to Be You—Session focused on discovering your authentic self.*
- *Lead Affirmed in Purpose*
- *Lead with Intention to Influence and Inspire*
- *Lead by Embracing Transformation and Serve*
- *Lead with Heart—A Focus on Emotional Intelligence*
- *Going Beyond Work-Life Balance to Ignite Passion and Thrive*
- *Women Seeking Balance to Thrive in Leadership and Life*
- *Selfcare is not Selfish: Healthy Means More Selfless*

Visit Sarah's website for more sessions or to book her for your next event.
sarahsajohnson.com

Sarah Johnson has served as an educational leader in Northwestern Wisconsin since 2003. She is a former English teacher and elementary, middle, and high school principal turned author, podcaster, and professional speaker. She is an adjunct professor for Viterbo University in the Educational Leadership Department and a supervisor of student teachers for edu-CATE-WI. In addition to *Lead with FAITH*, Sarah is also co-author of *Balance like a Pirate: Going Beyond Work-Life Balance to Ignite Passion and Thrive as an Educator* (2018). She holds a certificate for Women in Leadership from Cornell University and is pursuing district administrator licensure. Sarah passionately serves the In AWE community she has built through the *In AWE Podcast*, a weekly show where she amplifies women to empower a community through the mission in their messages. Sarah resides in a beautiful no stoplight town with her two daughters and teacher/coach husband. Connect with Sarah at sarahsajohnson.com or on any social media platform @sarahsajohnson.

www.ingramcontent.com/pod-product-compliance
Lightning Source LLC
Chambersburg PA
CBHW030323100526
44592CB00010B/543